S0-CFY-936

# With Integrity of Heart
## Living Values in Changing Times

## CLIFFORD ELLIOTT

**Friendship Press** • **New York**

Unless otherwise stated, all Bible quotations in this book are from the
New Revised Standard Version, copyright 1989 by the Division of Education and Ministry of the National Council of the Churches of Christ
in the U.S.A. In certain instances, where the reference is marked *,
quotations have been edited for inclusive language according to that organization's guidelines or edited for clarity in context. Other translations
are occasionally cited for comparison or as quoted in another publication.

© 1991 by Friendship Press
Editorial Offices:
475 Riverside Drive, Room 860, New York, NY 10115
Distribution Offices:
P.O. Box 37844, Cincinnati, OH 45222-0844

All rights reserved. No part of this book may be reproduced in any
manner whatsoever without the written permission of Friendship Press,
except brief quotations in critical articles or reviews.

Manufactured in the United States of America

**Library of Congress Cataloging-in-Publication Data**

Elliott, Clifford A. S. (Clifford Allan Stuart), 1919–
    With integrity of heart : living values in changing times /
Clifford Elliott.
        p.    cm.
    ISBN 0-377-00219-4
    1. Christian ethics—United Church of Canada authors.
2. Integrity.  3. Values.  4. Church and social problems.
I. Title.
BJ1251.E39  1991
241'.04792—dc20                                             91-289
                                                               CIP

To the many members who participated
in "Renewal of Faith" studies
at Metropolitan and Bloor Street United Churches, Toronto,
and who searched with me for the faith
that leads to living values

# Acknowledgments

I WANT TO THANK Friendship Press for giving me the opportunity to write this book. I found it a challenge to try to see the implications of Christian faith for both our broad view of the world and the way that worldview translates into the day-to-day moral decisions each of us has to make. I was painfully conscious of the magnitude of such a task, especially in a world so engulfed in turmoil and so torn with conflicting ideologies and moral standards. Many times I felt it was presumptuous even to attempt such a task. Yet I also felt that this is a task every Christian must undertake, and that each of us is called to make whatever contribution we can to this common challenge.

It was a help to have Audrey Miller, executive director of Friendship Press, and the Program Committee on Education for Mission choose the theme, "Living Values/Changing Times," and to share with me some preliminary ideas and concerns. Once I had written a draft of the book, some very long-suffering members of the committee spent hours — often vacation hours — ploughing through the material. They carefully noted matters that needed consideration, asked for clarification and raised questions that had not occurred to me.

Behind all this was the skillful hand, warm encouragement and irresistible good humor of Carol Ames. She is one of those rare editors who not only helps a writer express ideas clearly and concisely, but who understands the subject matter thoroughly and involves herself deeply in the whole process of thinking it through. Working closely with Carol was Don Parker-Burgard, meticulous editorial assistant.

I am also grateful to the denominational staff who help prepare leaders, who in turn prepare others to lead the studies of which this book is a part. Finally, I am mindful of the members of congregations of many different denominations spread throughout North America who commit themselves, year after year, to read, study, reflect and act together, so that the gospel of Jesus Christ might be better known and applied in our society. It is an honor to be a small part of their ongoing work for the Reign of God.

# Contents

# Where do our values come from?

A YOUNG MAN stayed after a church meeting some time ago and asked to talk with me. He and his wife, Susan, regularly attended church and were deeply concerned with social issues. But Robert was clearly upset. "My wife and I work hard all week," he said, "and when we come to church we are looking for comfort. But we don't get much — especially lately. All we seem to hear about is 'Star Wars.' "

I was somewhat taken aback at this outburst, especially from him. I replied that I hadn't felt we were riding the Star Wars issue, although it had certainly been mentioned several times recently because I felt that its development would only escalate the arms race. I said that we tried to balance our services to offer both challenge and comfort: "I'm sorry if you're finding them all challenge and no comfort."

Robert is an environmentalist and Susan had recently graduated in law. They have one young child. When Robert received his Ph.D., his only good job offer was in a midwestern city. Susan gave up her position as a junior partner in a Toronto law firm and they moved west. But the city was experiencing an economic slump and Susan was unable to find a position with a law firm. After two years she still could not foresee any immediate prospect of employment; meanwhile she was losing contact with her law firm in Toronto.

After much discussion they decided that Robert should give up his position and that they should move back to Toronto. There Susan was able to regain her position with her law firm, but Robert could find no employment in his field of environmental concerns. "But finally," he said, "I did get a job in a special research project. And guess who is funding it? Star Wars."

Now I understood why he was so upset. Robert had a sensitive conscience and a strong Christian faith. He was torn between his need for a job and his commitment to his faith. In earlier times, when society expected husbands to be the providers and wives to be the homemakers, the tension might have been prevented by the move to the Midwest: Susan would probably not have had a profession of her own. Now Robert was caught between wanting to affirm his wife's right to develop her career while needing to pursue his own as well. But the greatest tension arose in the conflict between his opposition to the arms race and his need for a job. It seemed impossible to be faithful to all his ideals.

Times had changed. Did he have to adjust his values to suit the changing times? As he thought about it, he realized that the changing times had been accompanied by some good changes in values — like increased recognition of women's right to pursue their careers, and a new concern for the environment. But new tensions came along with new values, as these clashed with old values not yet relinquished. But where did he get his values? Did he consciously choose them or just accept them from others? When one value is in conflict with another, how do you choose between them, or resolve the tension?

## The Challenge of Confusion

Robert and Susan's story of people caught in apparently impossible dilemmas because of changing times could be told a hundred times over. Stories can be told about the families of those who fish on the East coasts of Canada and the U.S. Larger boats, modern fishing methods and huge processing plants have depleted the fishing stocks. Obviously, strict quotas have to be put on the number of fish that can be caught. But that means closing fish plants, putting people out of work. It means deciding who will be allowed to keep jobs and who will lose them. On what basis would such a difficult decision be made?

Meanwhile, tension of another sort has developed in Goose Bay, Labrador, in Canada. There, military planes from several NATO countries practice low-level flights — about seven thousand of them a year. The native Innu people say that the deafening noise frightens their children and has a detrimental effect on the caribou. The noise threatens to destroy their whole way of life. Along with environmentalists they have protested vigorously and conducted sit-ins on the runways to prevent the planes from carrying out their runs. But Canadian military authorities say the flights are necessary for Canada to discharge its commitments to NATO. And the residents of Happy Valley-Goose Bay say that without the flights, and the economic benefits they bring, their town would die and hundreds of people would be thrown out of work. Is there any way to resolve this dilemma to bring justice to all? Times have changed. The flights at Goose Bay can no longer be defended simply as "progress." Progress, as a value, has been challenged in light of some of the human costs it entails.

"Progress" is also challenged in light of our new concern for nature. After centuries of using nature as a commodity for human beings to consume in any way they see fit, people are suddenly seeing that this attitude threatens their very survival. And there is no place to hide. The deforestation of the Amazon river basin affects every human being on the planet. So this deforestation must be stopped at once, we say. But Brazil says, "We need the land for farming and raising cattle. It means jobs and hard currency to help us pay our heavy foreign debt. You, who have used nature to bring about a higher standard of living for yourselves, can hardly condemn us for wanting to do the same for ourselves." Again, the changing times have brought about a conflict in values.

Meanwhile, a radical change has taken center stage in Eastern Europe. The destruction of the Berlin wall was a very dramatic symbol. It was an admission that communism, as it had been practiced in the Soviet Union and its satellites, had failed. But some in the West wondered how long it would be before some of these "liberated" people saw the gross inequities in *our* system — the high unemployment in many areas, the lack of medical care in some prosperous countries, the huge gap between the rich and the poor in nations that pride themselves on "equality of opportunity for all," the tremendous drive toward the consumption of material goods. Having abandoned the values of communism, might they begin to ask where we get our values? Might this be a time when East and West have to look together at their value systems, even be driven to do so by the radical political and social changes that are taking place?

The confusion and conflict in values that we are all experiencing challenge us to new visions of the values we might, in fact, embrace. Some leaders are taking up this challenge and urging us to imagine a new and different kind of world. Here is Eduard Shevardnadze, then foreign minister of the Soviet Union, speaking in October 1989 in the United States:

> We need...to begin a new life for ourselves.... It will be necessary to overcome a certain psychological barrier, to go beyond national concerns and to start thinking in global terms.... Courage is the most important thing in today's politics. Today it is not enough to be a realist who perceives life as it is. In addition, what is needed is vision and even idealism and a keen sense of novelty.[1]

And here is Stanley Hoffman, who chairs the Center for European Studies at Harvard University:

> There are periods of history when profound changes occur all of a sudden, and the acceleration of events is such that much of what experts write is obsolete before it gets into print. We are now in one of those periods, which obliges the U.S. to rethink its role in the world, just as it was forced to do by the cataclysmic changes that followed the end of the Second World War.... Now that global tensions are easing, a nation's interests can no longer be defined simply in reaction to those of "the enemy." Now that the enemy recedes, a redefinition of those interests becomes possible and necessary.... We cannot replace a fading vision — that of containment — with mere short-term management and avoidance of trouble/ because the present offers opportunities for a decisive change in direction and because there are simply too many dangers ahead to allow us to stumble from issue to issue in a pragmatic way.[2]

---

[1]Speaking to the Foreign Policy Association in New York. Reported in the *Washington Post* and reprinted in the *Manchester Guardian Weekly*, Oct. 15, 1989.
[2]*Atlantic Monthly*, October 1989.

Such challenges excite us. In the midst of our difficulties and despair in looking for values that apply in our day, it is good to have leaders from two regions of the world stimulate our imaginations to think globally, not just nationally, to think not just of realities but of possibilities, to risk making decisive changes in direction, not just stumble from issue to issue.

## Values from the Outside In

But before we look for visions that could provide values, we need to ask what we mean by values, and how we come to have them. Do we actually choose our values, or simply inherit them, or accept whatever values our culture provides or approves?

Carl Rogers, a professor of psychology and psychiatry, says that our value system begins in our infancy when we show a preference, in our actions, for one kind of object, or objective, rather than another. Infants, for example, value food when they are hungry, but reject it when they are full. Their system, therefore, is flexible, not fixed. Moreover, the source of their value system is within them. They are not influenced by what others want, only by what they like or dislike.

When we get a bit older, however, says Rogers, we find that some actions win approval, others disapproval.[3] If we want to win approval, we adopt another value system — one that pleases others. The values that we accept from others tend to be fixed or rigid, rather than fluid or flexible. They are seen as rules to be obeyed, patterns to be followed.

In time, although these values came from outside ourselves, we may accept them as our own. Usually we do this in order to be accepted or loved. Because these values have not emerged from our own experience we do not feel free to challenge them nor to have them challenged, because that might threaten our acceptance by the ones we most want to please. But because we have not chosen these values, we feel insecure about them and therefore cling to them all the more tenaciously.

We begin to mature, says Rogers, when we find the locus of values in ourselves, as we did when we were infants — when we value our own experience and can stand against the values of

---

[3]Carl Rogers and Barry Stevens, *Person to Person: The Problem of Being Human* (Moab, Utah: Real People Press, 1967).

others if we need to. Choices, however, are much more complex than they were when we were infants. Choices involve the learnings of the past and take into account the experiences of others. Mature choices are always a blend of old truths and new insights.

This process may set up severe inner tensions when several conflicting choices or values commend themselves to us. Or tension may arise if the way we choose is in conflict with the way others have chosen for us — others whom we respect and whose love we need.

Such a conflict is dramatized in the film "Dead Poets Society." A teenager is sent by his father to an expensive school to prepare to study medicine. The father, who never had such an opportunity, has sacrificed a great deal to send his son to the school; it never occurs to him that his son might choose another vocation. In time, however, as the son is exposed to poetry and drama, he tells his father he wants to become an actor. When the father insists on the original plan, the son is torn. Whose vision shall he follow: his own or his father's? His inner torment leads him to end his life tragically.

Rogers believes that we all have within us "an organismic basis for valuing." If we can learn to be in touch with this valuing process, he says, we will behave in ways that are self-enhancing and that also enhance others and the whole human race. He believes that this process leads, in all cultures, to common values — values like sincerity and self-direction, but also values like social responsibility and loving interpersonal relationships.[4]

Rogers's approach helps us understand why we suppress our own inner instincts and insights and accept the values prescribed by others. We all want to be liked. Many of us doubt our own convictions, often with good reason, or lack the courage to affirm them when we are in a minority. But we know, too, how insecure we feel when we accept others' patterns without much examination, simply to conform. Christians know how often the Bible has been used as an external authority rather than as an inner resource, and how both the Bible and the believer have been diminished in the process. We welcome contemporary theologians like Elisabeth Schüssler Fiorenza who urge us to approach Scripture "as nourishing bread rather than as unchanging sacred word

---

[4]Ibid., p. 28.

engraved in stone."[5] We realize why we have sometimes clung so tenaciously to certain verses or particular interpretations of the Bible, rather than allowing ourselves to be open to whatever it might teach us.

*So who knows?* // But Rogers's approach is limited by the implication that we hold within ourselves all the resources we need to develop a valid value system. He seems certain that if the right process is followed — by constantly looking within ourselves and trusting the insights we get there — we will arrive at values that will be valid not only for ourselves but for the whole human race. Not everyone is that confident. They look for something more transcendent. Even Mikhail Gorbachev, when visiting the pope, said: "We need spiritual values.... We need to rethink man's attitude toward nature, other people and himself. We need a revolution of the mind."// Somehow we doubt that we will discover truly spiritual values, experience a radical rethinking of our former attitudes and achieve a "revolution of the mind" simply by further exploration of our own experience. *Amen!*

## Faith and Belief

For Christians, values grow out of our faith as well as our experience. The connection is even closer: our values are inseparable from our faith. I speak of *faith* rather than *belief* because the word *belief* has changed from its original meaning.[6] *Belief* comes from an old English word meaning "to hold dear" or "to prize." It comes from the same root as the word *love*. A belief, then, once meant something that one loved, to which one was deeply committed. Today belief has come to mean "to have an opinion" about something. For example, to say "I believe in God" may, for some, mean only "I believe there is a God" or "I believe in the existence of God." But originally to say "I believe in God" meant that I love God and am committed with all my heart to God.

Similarly, *creed* comes from the Latin *credo*, which means, "I set my heart" on something. For us it has often come to mean instead, "to give intellectual assent to a set of doctrines."

---

[5] Elisabeth Schüssler Fiorenza, "Changing the Paradigms," *Christian Century*, September 5–12, 1990.

[6] As Wilfred Cantwell Smith points out so well in his books *Belief and History* (Charlottesville: University Press of Virginia, 1977) and *Faith and Belief* (Princeton, N.J.: Princeton University Press, 1979).

A belief, then, is centered in the heart and is more than an opinion or an intellectual matter. But it is important to realize that for the Hebrews and for the early Christians the "heart" was more than the seat of the emotions. It included the whole of one's being — all of what we divide into heart, mind, soul and will. To believe something was to give it one's *whole* heart, one's very *self*. Jesus emphasizes this when he says that we should love God with all our heart, soul, mind — and *strength* (Mark 12:30). Or, as we might put it, "with all our *might.*"//Our ultimate belief — and our highest value — is not only what we live by but what we would die for.\

Our first question then is: "How deeply am I committed to what I say I value? Is it a matter of life and death to me? If it is not, what is ultimately most important to me? To what (or whom) have I given my heart?" If we can identify what that is, we will know what lies at the heart of our value system.

The answer will raise the next question: "Is it worth it? Have I set my heart on something of secondary importance?" That is, if the "bottom line" for me is: "How much money will it bring me?" or "Will it give me power over others?" or "Will it make me more popular?" I may well question my priorities. Have I given my heart to something that is ultimately not worth it? As Jesus put it: "What will it profit people to gain the whole world and forfeit their life? Indeed, what can they give in return for their life?" (Mark 8:36–37*). The only thing Jesus sees as worth giving one's life for is "the gospel." Each of us must decide, then, what "the gospel" is for us.

## God's Kind of Love

Here again our faith, our belief, must be centered in something beyond and greater than ourselves, greater than others, greater than any institution or code of conduct. All these will contribute to our faith, positively or negatively. But the center must be nothing less than God. While God is ultimately beyond our comprehension, we believe that God's central character has been made known to us in certain acts of history, especially as recorded in the Bible, in the lives of prophets and saints and supremely in the life and teachings of Jesus. We dare to believe that the central characteristic of God is love — not just any kind of love but the quality of love we see in Jesus Christ. This love becomes both source and guide as we choose and judge our values. A New Testament writer said to his people:

> I pray that, according to the riches of God's glory, God may grant that you may be strengthened in your inner being with power through God's Spirit, and *that Christ may dwell in your hearts through faith, as you are being rooted and grounded in love.* I pray that you may have the power to comprehend, with all the saints, what is the breadth and length and height and depth, and to know the love of Christ that surpasses knowledge, so that you may be filled with all the fullness of God (Ephesians 3:16–19*; emphasis added).[7]

Here the writer recognizes that we need values that transcend any we might merely choose for ourselves, values rooted and grounded in the love of Christ. But the writer also recognizes that such transcendent values transcend our own abilities. Yet that recognition leads us not into despair but into hope as we pray for God to empower us in our inner beings. Only in the assurance that God's loving Spirit is at work in us can we dare to take the ultimate leap of faith — to give our hearts to loving as God loves. As another writer put it: "We love because God first loved us" (1 John 4:19*).

When God's love becomes our ultimate value we are not being guided by an abstraction. God's love is always concrete, expressed in specific acts, particular kinds of people and relationships. Though God's love uses laws to give us more specific direction, God's laws are always more than a set of rules. God's law is expressed in a certain kind of spirit. Instead of being a burden imposed from without, God's law becomes a loving hand that guides us on our way. So the Psalmist can say to God, "Your law is my delight," and exclaim, "Oh, how I love your law!" (Psalm 119:77, 97). For the Psalmist, to obey God's law is not merely to make certain specific decisions in response to particular commandments. God's law helps form a *pattern* of choosing, a *way* of making decisions.

---

[7]An asterisk has been added to those scriptural references where the passage has been modified, e.g., for inclusive language. See page ii.

God's kind of love, which we believe in, which we cherish, which we "hold dear," is never static, never rigid. Like a Spirit blowing into the sail of our lives, it carries us to our destination.

This Spirit is also a certain quality of life by which we test other qualities. We know that all that we value is not necessarily "good." Nor are values that may be good enough in themselves worthy of devoting our heart to. That is why we are warned that "the love of money is the root of all kinds of evil, and in their eagerness to be rich some have wandered away from the faith and pierced themselves with many pains" (1 Timothy 6:10). Money, in itself, may be valued for good reasons or be used for valuable ends, but when we love it, are devoted to it as an end in itself, it becomes an idol. Its potential good is turned into evil. In the light of the Spirit of God's love, the worship of money is seen to be the worship of a false god and therefore to be of negative value.

Finally, God's love is not simply a reservoir from which we can continue to draw values and guidance. It is more like a fountain which, flowing from a living God, always brings values that are fresh, that are expressed in new and living ways (see John 4:14). It is like a spring that flows from God's heart to our hearts. "The heart is above all the central place ... to which God turns, where religious experience has its root, which determines conduct."[8] We work out our values as we speak with God "heart to heart."

## Setting Our Course

If we link our values so closely to our faith, we need to examine our faith at the same time that we examine our values. In the first chapter of this book we will consider the all-too-common experience in which people value themselves poorly. Why do many people who seem to have everything think they are worthless? What kind of faith would enable us to love ourselves in the best sense?

In chapter 2 we will push this question further. We will consider the forces around us, expressed particularly in the media, that seem to treat us as commodities, as consumers. How can we learn to define ourselves rather than accept others' definitions of us?

---

[8]G. Kittel, *Theologisches Worterbuch zum Neuen Testament* 3:615, quoted by E. C. Blackman, in *A Theological Word Book of the Bible*, ed. Alan Richardson (London: SCM Press, 1957), p. 144.

In chapter 3 we will consider the cynicism and despair that are so widespread in our society. Where and how can we find a faith that will give us hope?

In chapter 4 we will examine what happens in a society that values "private enterprise" and individual endeavor so highly that the ideal of community withers. How can we learn to support one another in our common task of coping with a world so full of change?

In chapter 5 we will look at what takes place in our lives when competing demands and duties seem to tear us apart. Even demands that are good in themselves can overwhelm our time and energy. How do we choose what we ought to do? How do we find some sense of wholeness, of integration?

In the last chapter we will turn again to visions and hopes for the future, for ourselves and our world. How do our own aspirations fit into those visions?

We will not expect to arrive at simple or easy decisions. We will recognize how difficult and complex many choices will be. We will acknowledge that often choices seem to be made for us. Sometimes, even when we think we are making a clear choice, we may have been so conditioned by our upbringing or our culture that we cannot distinguish clearly between what we have been taught and what we consciously choose. We will be aware how often several good values conflict with one another and make it difficult to establish priorities.

Some of this complexity and conflict is illustrated by the situations mentioned briefly earlier in this Introduction. How, for example, do people who have depended all their lives on fishing for their own and their families' livelihood "choose" to do something different when the fishing stocks are depleted? How do we tell people in Goose Bay, who would become unemployed if the NATO base were removed, that they must not worship jobs? How does Robert, who works, against his conscience, for a Star Wars project, resolve his inner conflict? We realize that the choice of values is complex and that choosing can be very costly.

Such dilemmas make it all the more necessary to set our hearts on something that transcends our particular time and situation. In fact, we cannot understand "where we are" unless we can rise above "where we are" and envision things "as they should be" or as they can be. This vision, of course, reveals a gap between hard facts and high hopes, but that gap can become, by faith, a creative tension rather than a destructive one.

Someone has said that we are now in the situation of a navigator who has lost confidence in the ship's compass and even in the stars. We have discovered much about our natural world, but that knowledge does not give us guidance for a course to follow right now. Are we then reduced to taking soundings by hand and just feeling our way, step by step and day by day? Or is there some way we can look again at the stars, find our bearings, set our course and commit ourselves in faith to it?

Our very search for what gives meaning and purpose — and joy — to life is what distinguishes us as children of God. And we are not alone in our search. Along the way we meet others and join them in our quest. We learn from their experiences, their cultures, their history, as well as from our own. We will make mistakes and may have to make compromises. But we will be aware that in all this, our loving God is not keeping a scorecard but working with us. Our objective is not moral perfection, even if that were attainable, but purity of heart. Purity of heart has to do with singleness of purpose or, as Søren Kirkegaard defined it: "Purity of heart is to will one thing."

Here is the way one psalmist describes it:

> I will sing of loyalty and of justice;
> to you, O Lord, I will sing.
> I will study the way that is blameless.
> When shall I attain it?
>
> I will walk with integrity of heart within my house;
> I will not set before my eyes anything that is base.
>
> (Psalm 101:1–3)

Here is someone who wants to be loyal to what is just, to find a way that is true, to reject what is false and, above all, to "walk with integrity of heart." And that, I would say, is something to sing about.

# 1

*guilty*
*failures*

*children*
*of God*

# How do we value ourselves?

F OR TWENTY YEARS as a pastor I conducted "Renewal of Faith" classes. A group of ten to fifteen people would gather for eight to ten weeks to discuss their faith. The classes were intended to help people in their spiritual journeys and were open to both church members and nonmembers.

Many who came to these gatherings were middle-class people who appeared to be accomplished and fulfilled but who felt an emptiness at the core of their lives. These basically "good" people did not feel "good" — they felt guilty or felt they had failed in some way to live up to the expectations of others, of God or of themselves.

Sandra was a woman in her middle thirties. (I have not used real names and the persons described are not actual persons but "composite characters" that personify the kinds of people who attended the classes.) Though she had been raised in a church-going home, she left the church in her early teens. Leaving the church was partly a way to rebel against her parents and partly a way to do what her friends were doing. At university, Sandra became an agnostic, although she was active in social causes. After graduating with a degree in social work she took a job in which her chief responsibility was counseling teenagers. She married and had two children. Life seemed enjoyable, challenging and fulfilling.

When Sandra's marriage felt apart she was shocked. Although she wasn't quite sure what had caused the failure, she was left with a feeling of uneasiness akin to guilt. Divorce left her lonely.

And inadequate. She had custody of the two children and being a single parent was hard work. There wasn't enough money to meet their growing needs. The teenagers she counseled seemed increasingly difficult to help; many were runaways now into drugs and prostitution. Exhausted at day's end, she faced new responsibilities at home. Life seemed empty at its center, no longer enjoyable or fulfilling. Moral values, like concern for the environment, seemed only to lay yet more responsibility on her. Weary and frustrated and short-tempered with her children, Sandra wondered whether she was a failure as a mother as well as in marriage.

For the first time in years, Sandra felt the need for some kind of living faith, some inner spiritual resource to sustain her in all these pressures. Above all, she needed to increase her own self-acceptance. But how could she go about doing that?

She looked back on her parents' lives. While she felt many of their views were simply out-of-date they had, she knew, always found a certain stability and serenity in their faith. What if she were to go back to the church? Would it have anything to offer? She decided to go and see.

Now she sat with a group of fifteen people in our discussion/study group. At first she was wary. Was this class a subtle way of coating the pill of certain doctrines to get people to swallow what they really didn't believe? At first she just sat there, determined, it seemed, not to say much till she had sized up the class.

When she did speak she said: "One thing I can't bear right now is a judgmental God. The God I rejected was always making impossible demands and was slow to forgive those who failed to live up to them. It was a God who always made me feel guilty, always made me feel like a failure. I didn't need that then and I certainly don't need it now. Many days I feel I've failed in my marriage, failed as a mother, failed in my job, failed as a citizen. Does anybody else feel that way?"

Eleanor, a woman about Sandra's age, spoke up about her dilemma. A single person, without a family, she seemed to have everything going for her. She worked in a bank and was obviously doing well. Management, anxious that the public see that the bank gave women positions of executive responsibility, saw Eleanor's potential and were promoting her quickly.

But Eleanor was hesitant. She was being groomed, she felt, for "the top." But what was the top, and why should she strive for it? Management obviously intended that executives should put the bank first. A personal life was to come second. More than that, she had some inner misgivings about her own success. Was she really that good or had she just happened to come along at the right time? Did she really have what it takes to assume leadership or was she basically a "phony," able to project the right image to mask a very ordinary person? Could some looming event strip that façade away and expose her for "what she really was" — artificial props and all?

Eleanor's parents had always held up high standards for her and by hard work she had been able to meet them. But what if the expectations were now just too high? Some days it would be a relief if someone said: "We've made a mistake. We know who you really are. We think it is better for you and for all concerned if you resign immediately."

Eleanor could relate to Sandra not so much through a feeling of guilt as through her feeling of inadequacy. She, too, was looking for some inner spiritual resources to ground a "real" self. She, too, was carrying unbearable burdens.

And then there was Michael. He was a little older, in his middle forties. Michael listened to Eleanor and said, with some bitterness in his voice, "I wish I had your problem. You're on the way *up*. I'm on the way *out*. In fact, I am already out. After fifteen years of steady promotions in my business I'm out of a job. Our firm was taken over by another but I thought that, as a vice-president, my future was assured. I was wrong. Our whole division was dismissed. I got a severance package, and I thought with my record and references I would have no trouble getting another position. That's six months ago. After countless applications I've had exactly one set of interviews. My wife and children are patient and supportive but I feel sort of lost. Every time I come home I check the mail or the answering machine to see if anyone has returned my enquiries. My days are empty. I'm trying to fill them by repairing my garage. This at least gives me some tangible sense of accomplishment. But as I hammer away at the nails and saw the boards I ask myself: 'Who am I anyway? Just a washed-up failure? A nobody who masqueraded as a somebody for fifteen years?'"

### "Be Ye Perfect"

When I first listened to people like Sandra, Eleanor and Michael,
I blamed this sense of failure entirely on their early religious upbringing. I believed them when they said they had been taught
to believe in a God of judgment who made them feel they were
guilty. But then I began to realize that other influences were at
work as well. The secular world had imposed these influences:
the pressures to succeed, to achieve, to get to the top, which left
people feeling that even their best was not good enough.

Recently I was reminded of these classes when I read *The
Impostor Syndrome: When Success Makes You Feel Like a Fake*, by
Pauline Clance, professor of psychology at Georgia State University. In her research and in her practice as a psychotherapist,
Dr. Clance kept meeting people who had every reason to be on
top of the world but who felt miserable because in their own
eyes they never measured up. Filled with fears and self-doubts,
these people suffer from what Dr. Clance calls "The Impostor Phenomenon." They feel that they are not what they appear to be or
pretend to be, so they live in constant anxiety and fear of being
"found out."[1]

Clance believes that more than half the population experiences
impostor feelings from time to time. People who do so are often
perfectionists, like Eleanor, who feel that they are expected not
only to do well but to excel. Perhaps their parents told them so,
in words or by attitude. Or perhaps their employers or colleagues
imply it by their very compliments and promotions. To meet their
own expectations such people may become overly conscientious or
even workaholics. But nothing they do ever seems quite enough.
Moreover, they may say to themselves or others, "I'm not really
very gifted or I wouldn't have to work so hard to accomplish my
goals."

Or, like Sandra, people may wonder if they are attempting too
much. Women whose mothers stayed at home and looked after
their families may feel guilty for having broken that pattern. Having achieved more than they ever expected in one field, they feel
guilty for achieving less in another. Men, on the other hand, may
feel the only way to prove oneself is in business or a profession.

---

[1]Pauline Clance, *The Impostor Syndrome: When Success Makes You Feel Like a
Fake* (New York: Bantam Books, 1986; Atlanta: Peachtree Publishers, 1985).

So long as he was moving up the corporate ladder, Michael felt he was a success, he could accept himself. But once he lost his job, he felt he was of no value.

Paradoxically, our feelings of guilt or inadequacy can be used to buttress our need for self-acceptance. One of Ellen Goodman's characters says, "Maybe that's it. We can lead lives different from our mothers or our colleagues so long as we feel guilty about it. Guilt is the scrap we throw to the past. It's the way we acknowledge the 'shoulds' of our childhood." After all, says Goodman, "anyone who feels guilty isn't a truly bad person.... If we gave up feeling guilty, like smoking or eating meat... we might have to take up running instead."[2]

Christians, ironically, are especially good at this game. Strange, is it not, that many self-respecting Christians are reluctant to call themselves Christians? To do so might imply that they had achieved a degree of moral perfection that no one but Jesus Christ had achieved. Yet we all feel that we "ought to be" Christians and that we are, indeed, expected by God to be just that. Being a Christian thus becomes an unbearable burden, relieved only by denying that we are "really" Christians. Unwittingly, those of us who call on others to be Christians may be laying on them an impossible demand. "Thou shalt be a Christian" becomes an eleventh commandment. To people who feel they have already failed to keep the original Ten Commandments, that is indeed bad news, an invitation to increased guilt, to greater self-rejection.

## Gods That Fail

Obviously, no one can live for long with such feelings. So we try different remedies. One solution for a sense of worthlessness offered by our secular society is to make lots of money. Those with a lot of money are judged, and can judge themselves, as "persons of considerable worth." This is not a new phenomenon. Lewis Lapham, editor of *Harper's* magazine, says: "The history of the United States is synonymous with the dream of riches."[3] He claims that the Puritans who settled the New England colonies managed to join virtue with the making of money, thus melding

---

[2]Ellen Goodman, *At Large* (New York: Summit Books, 1981), pp. 78–79.

[3]*Money and Class in America: Notes and Observations on the Civil Religion* (New York: Ballantine, 1989), p. 36.

moral worth with material worth: "They assigned spiritual meaning to the texts of money and conceived of their New Jerusalem
as a real-estate development in which God and Mammon held an
equal interest."[4]

Worship of such an ideal, such a god, Lapham maintains, continues to this day; it reached its peak in the Reagan era. He quotes
the former president as saying, "What I want to see above all is
that this remains a country where someone can always get rich."[5]

Unfortunately for many who trusted in money to supply self-
esteem, this god has failed them. Says Lapham: "Never in the
history of the world have so many people been so rich; never in
the history of the world have so many of these same people felt
themselves so poor. It is an odd paradox."[6]

Lapham tells of meeting a friend he had not seen for thirty
years. The man was making $250,000 a year. "I'm nothing," he
said. "You understand that, nothing. I earn $250,000 a year, but
it's nothing, and I'm nobody."[7] Because this man had developed a
way of living that always demanded more than he made, he kept
redefining his own "poverty line," and never rose above it.

Such people experience chagrin and anger at having been be-
trayed. "Imagining that they [could] be transformed into gods,
they find themselves changed into dwarfs.... Seeking the invisible through the imagery of the visible, the Americans never can
get quite all the way to the end of the American dream."[8]

If the rich feel this way, how do middle-class people feel? According to Barbara Ehrenreich, not much better. In *Fear of Falling:
The Inner Life of the Middle Class*, she describes the intellectual,
political and moral journey of the professional middle class from
the 1960s to the 1980s.[9] While they earn more money than the
great majority of people, their sense of security and worth has tra-
ditionally been grounded on more than income. It has depended
on their ideals, their ability to pursue those ideals in their vocations, their hard work and self-discipline. But, says Ehrenreich,

---

[4]Ibid., p. 36.
[5]Ibid., p. 8.
[6]Ibid., p. 7.
[7]Ibid., p. 9.
[8]Ibid., pp. 30–31.
[9]Barbara Ehrenreich, *Fear of Falling: The Inner Life of the Middle Class* (New
York: Pantheon Books, 1989).

they have become an insecure and deeply anxious elite. They are afraid of falling, of inner weakness, of growing soft, failing to strive, losing their discipline and will. They have, she says, tended to trade vocations for mere jobs. Having lost the satisfaction that comes from pursuing their ideals in their work, they have tried to find fulfillment in consuming. "We need a revival of consciousness and responsibility in the middle-class," says Ehrenreich.[10]

## Outside the Mainstream

If a feeling of low self-worth is common among middle-class people and among the rich, what about those who are not in the mainstream of society, people who may be considered more or less marginalized for a variety of reasons? Do they escape the pressures and anxieties of the "mainstream" or do they feel as insecure about themselves as Sandra and Michael and others in the Renewal of Faith class? Do they feel, like Lapham's rich friend, that they are nobodies? Unfortunately, it would appear that they do not escape these feelings of self-rejection. In fact, if there is one thing all classes of people seem to share, it is feelings of guilt and failure.

Here is a man we will call Lorne. He is a Native Indian. Reluctant to expose him to another culture at a young age, his parents delayed sending him to school until he was eleven. Then other students laughed at him; inevitably, fights broke out. The school principal always seemed to blame Lorne. After a year and a half at school, Lorne was glad when his father took him out and put him to work in a logging camp. He was a good worker and in a few years was doing the work of a man.

At seventeen he married. He says that he had always felt inferior because he was an Indian and so he thought marrying a white woman would bring him more acceptance. The marriage went reasonably well until his wife wanted to have children. When they were unable to do so, Lorne automatically assumed that it was his fault. Feeling all the more inferior, he started to drink to ease the pain. His wife asked him to choose between her and alcohol. He made his choice and drifted away.

Before long he was sorry and came home to try and be reconciled to his wife. He was arrested on the spot and charged with

---

[10]Ibid., p. 251.

nonsupport, not only of his wife but of the child she was bearing, fathered by another man. Lorne flew into a rage, refused to pay and went off on another drinking bout.

This pattern continued for many years. Sober, Lorne would try to start life anew, only to slip back into hopelessness and self-hate. It was a long time before he could accept himself as an Indian, as an alcoholic and as just plain Lorne.

Bob's background is entirely different from Lorne's but he, too, has been forced out of the mainstream. Bob is in his early forties and works for a magazine for gay people. He is gay and is a volunteer "buddy" to a man who has AIDS. His mother has never accepted his sexual orientation and some years ago, mostly to please her, he got married. The marriage did not work well and after a few years he and his wife separated. Bob felt called to become a minister and had begun his theological training. But when his marriage broke up, he left his seminary training and worked in a variety of jobs. But the call to the ministry simply would not go away. He wants to return to the seminary, but when he told his bishop he was homosexual the bishop did not even reply to his application.

Now he feels he is living in a kind of limbo. At times he lashes out against God: "Why do you keep calling me to ministry and then put up roadblocks that prevent me from answering your call?" Some days it is all he can do to preserve any self-respect. It is tempting to accept the rejection of his mother and his bishop and feel he is at best a second-class person.

Marlene grew up in poverty. She was sexually abused at home from the time she was six years old until she was thirteen. Her stepfather was a bootlegger, and Marlene was shunned by her playmates at school, not knowing why. At sixteen, when she became pregnant, she married Don, the father of her child. To their great sadness, the child was found to have a mental disability. Marlene's mother, a devout woman, told Marlene it was God's judgment on her for becoming pregnant before she got married. She said it so many times that Marlene finally believed her.

Meantime, Marlene and Don had seven children; two died in infancy. Don was not able to hold a job and they often had to depend on welfare. Don would cash the monthly check, then spend whatever he wished on beer and give Marlene the rest. He forbade her to leave the house and told her she was good for nothing but to cook and look after him and the children. Finally he left her. She had nothing but welfare to support herself and the family, but even worse, she had absolutely no self-confidence. She had believed what her husband told her about herself.

Lorne, Bob and Marlene are all afflicted with a feeling of low self-worth. Lorne feels he is inferior because of his race, a race that whites told him was inferior. Bob finds it hard to accept himself when all the "authority figures" — his mother and the church — reject him. Marlene feels she is rejected by God because her mother told her she was. She feels of no worth because her husband told her so.

These people, though "marginalized" in one sense, share the low self-image of "mainstream" people. Like Sandra, Marlene has had to struggle against accepting standards set by a parent and by an "inherited" concept of God. Both Lorne's rejection because of his race and Bob's because of his sexual orientation are set by society — as is Michael's stereotype that a man must be successful in business.

Lorne and Bob and Marlene are all "real people" with whom I have talked at length. I met them in the course of some research I was doing on how "marginalized" people cope and how we can better communicate with them.[11] I began by assuming that their values and their feelings would be different from my middle-class values and feelings. I found they were surprisingly similar. I began by assuming that the spiritual needs of people outside the church might be different from those inside the church. I found they were much the same. So many of us suffer from feelings of guilt, failure and inadequacy.

## The Business of Self-Esteem

The question now is: What can be done about it? Is there any hope, or are we all condemned to live out our lives with a constant sense of letting ourselves and others — and God — down? This is fundamentally a question of values. Can we find a way to value ourselves? What kind of faith would inspire a feeling of

---

[11]I have changed the names of these people but their stories are "true" stories. I have reduced them from much fuller versions, which I recorded in a book, *Speaking for Themselves: Hearing the Gospel from the Dispossessed, the Undervalued and the Marginalized* (Toronto: United Church Publishing House, and Nashville: Abingdon Press, 1990).

self-worth? How can we come to believe in ourselves, to "hold ourselves dear" in the original meaning of *belief*?[12]

First, we need to realize that the secular world is as aware as Christians of this question. It knows that the question reflects a profound need. Indeed, there are many who, realizing how deep and how widespread is this need, are able to make a lot of money by offering solutions.

The other day a flyer arrived in my mail. On the front cover, the bold, dramatic print said: "Break out of Jail!" It went on to promise: "The way to break out of your psychological jailhouse and achieve success beyond your wildest dreams is explained in 8 simple words.... To be a winner, think like a winner!" To develop a "psychology of winning" I need only order six cassettes (on free thirty-day trial). The course is obviously an example of the positive-thinking school, as shown by the first three of ten steps: (1) Positive self-expectancy; (2) Positive self-motivation; (3) Positive self-image. The final two lessons "suggest strategic applications for these attitudes and principles in the decades to come." They are called "Winning Keys for the Twenty-first Century," parts one and two.

In this course I am promised that "It doesn't take long. These self-training audiotapes work fast. Your free 30-day trial period will prove that you can soon be soaring with the eagles... achieving your 'impossible' dreams...and becoming one of those rare people *who almost always wins!*"

The flyer acknowledges that times have changed and that people cannot be as assured of lifetime security as they used to be. It speaks of "Mergers. Acquisitions. Breakdown of values. Budgets in crisis. The growing drug scene. This leaves you little you can count on...except uncertainty. *But you can always count on yourself.*"

Clearly, this enterprise is aimed at people who labor under self-doubt and low self-esteem. It promises to replace those negative qualms by changing their attitudes. One can see how such a proposal would be attractive to many people. Not only does it promise them everything they want to be and have; it assures them that they can do it all by themselves, with step-by-step guidance.

---

[12]See above p. 7.

Perhaps techniques of positive thinking would help some people raise themselves out of their self-doubt. But one wonders what such a technique would do for Sandra or Eleanor or thousands like them, to say nothing of what it would do for Lorne or Bob or Marlene. And the man who was already earning a quarter of a million dollars a year might well burst out in rage. We can hear him saying: "I did all the things you recommend and it has made me a winner in many people's eyes. But I feel it is all nothing and that I am nobody. Do you hear me? Nobody!"

Perhaps such approaches are aimed more at people like Michael, who has been a winner and now worries about becoming a loser. But Michael has already screwed up his courage and knocked on many doors, armed with the confidence that as a former successful vice-president he did have what it takes. But it hasn't worked so far.

Actually, both positive thinking and negative thinking are plagued by the same deficiency. Both are escapes from reality. Negative thinking is an escape into pessimism and positive thinking is an escape into optimism. As pessimism leaves no room for success, so optimism leaves no room for failure. Deep in our hearts we know that life is a mixture of success and failure and that we are a mixture of good and bad. What we need is a way to face that reality squarely.

## Starting Points

A more realistic approach is taken by psychotherapists like Pauline Clance. It suggests that we start by admitting our feelings to others. Just to find, as Sandra found in her discussion group, that we are not alone in such feelings can be reassuring. Then the Clance school suggests that we confront the thinking behind our claims of failure and guilt. One way of doing so is to list our actual achievements. In this we might need help from others since we may be used to hiding our achievements in order to justify our feelings of failure. Finally, we can learn to set realistic goals. One simple way to guarantee feelings of guilt and failure is to set, or to allow others to set for us, unrealistic goals; we are bound to fail in reaching them.

Such advice can help us to come to terms with our feelings of guilt and failure, especially when such feelings are unwarranted. It will come as a relief to see ourselves as better than we thought we were. But do we not want something more than that? I sensed, looking around the room at the people who came to the Renewal of Faith studies, that they were seeking not only a higher opinion of themselves but grounding in some source from beyond themselves. When we begin to talk in these terms we have entered the realm of religious faith, faith in God, since (as we have seen in the Introduction) it is possible to have other kinds of faith.

But where do we start? As we think of our sense of guilt and failure we are led to ask: "Guilty of what? Failure in relation to what? What are the standards against which we are measuring our actions? Where did we get those standards?" In most cases we find that we got these standards from someone else — from parents, from society, from religion, from friends. We may even have chosen them ourselves but without realizing the presuppositions behind the standards. Or having chosen them sincerely, we may feel they need re-examining.

### In the Beginning...

Carl Rogers, as we have seen, urges us to go back to our infancy so that we can recover a center that is based in ourselves rather than in others. But is there some way that we can go back even further than our own infancy — go back to our beginnings as human beings seeking and struggling with values? It is in origins that we often find meanings; significantly, the Bible begins with a book called "Genesis" — "beginnings." Here is how it starts:

> In the beginning when God created the heavens and the earth, the earth was a formless void and darkness covered the face of the deep, while a mighty wind from God swept over the face of the waters. Then God said, "Let there be light"; and there was light. And God saw that the light was good; and God separated the light from the darkness. God called the light Day, and the darkness God called Night. And there was evening and there was morning, the first day (Genesis 1:1–5*).

Then God continues to create further order out of chaos. The heavens are separated from the earth, the water is separated from the land and plant life begins. At each stage, "God saw that it was good."

Now comes the creation of the sun, moon and stars, giving a rhythm to day and night, seasons and years. Then God makes creatures that swim in the waters and birds that fly in the air, each, like the plants, with the power to reproduce its species. Then come animals of every kind to roam the earth. And again God "saw that it was good."

On the sixth day of creation human life appears:

> Then God said, "Let us make humankind in our image, according to our likeness; and let them have dominion over the fish of the sea, and over the birds of the air, and over the cattle, and over all the wild animals of the earth, and over every creeping thing that creeps upon the earth."

> > So God created humankind in God's image,
> > in the image of God, God created them;
> > male and female God created them.

> God blessed them, and God said to them, "Be fruitful and multiply, and fill the earth and subdue it; and have dominion over the fish of the sea and over the birds of the air and over every living thing that moves upon the earth." God said, "See, I have given you every plant yielding seed that is upon the face of all the earth, and every tree with seed in its fruit; you shall have them for food. And to every beast of the earth, and to every bird of the air, and to everything that creeps on the earth, everything that has the breath of life, I have given every green plant for food." And it was so. God saw everything that God had made, and indeed, it was very good" (Genesis 1:26–30*).

In this chapter, we need to hear not only how the *world* began, but also how *we* began, because the two beginnings are inseparable. And we are talking here more about the *meaning* of the beginning than the process. In the two verses that specifically describe the creation of human beings, it is stated *three times* that we were created *"in the image of God."*

> Then God said, "Let us make humankind in our own image, according to our likeness...." So God created humankind in

God's image, in the image of God, God created them; male
and female God created them (vv. 26–27*).

The word *image* does not mean merely "resemblance." It is
closer to the idea of "duplicate." Nor does image refer only to
our spiritual or intellectual nature; it does not shy away from
the thought of humans being like God in body as well as spirit.
In fact, the Hebrews did not make a body-spirit distinction. The
point is that human beings are like God in the way in which they
are called into existence, in the totality of their being.[13]
What, then, is the picture, the image of God, that is portrayed
in this first chapter of Genesis? The very first verse gives the answer: "In the beginning God *created*..." (RSV). In Genesis 1 we
learn that God creates, that God speaks, that God has a sense
of order and beauty. There is no declaration (except, possibly, by
implication) that God is all-wise or all-powerful. It does not even
say that God is loving. It is the *creator* God we see at work here.
And human beings are made in the image of this creator God.
By clear implication, therefore, the fundamental characteristic of
being human is to be creative. We are made with the creative
capacity to fulfill the tasks for which God creates us.

## Original Goodness

The other statement repeated in Genesis 1 is that at each stage
God stood back, as it were, and looked at what had been created. "And God saw everything that God had made, and indeed,
it was very good" (v. 31*). There is no doubt that God's created
goodness includes human beings. But goodness here does not imply mere moral goodness — God saw that the light was good and
that the trees were good and that the animals were good and that
everything God had made was good. The meaning we get here is
that everything God created, including human beings, turned out
the way God intended, the way God planned.
We note one other point about this story, this hymn, of the beginning of the earth. The writer is more theologian than historian
or scientist. The writer intends to tell us not only what happened
"in the beginning" but what is happening in creation all the time.
God creates order out of chaos, light out of darkness, life out of

---

[13]Gerhard von Rad, *Genesis* (Philadelphia: Westminster, 1973), p. 59.

matter. And God continues to make human beings in the image of God. That is *our* beginning. As Old Testament scholar Gerhard Von Rad puts it: "When Israel talked of the creation and ordering of the cosmos, she was discussing matters that were topical for [human beings] living here and now."[14]

In relation to our own self-image, when we go back to our ultimate origins, we come to a person made in the image of God, born creative, born "good," as God intended. We are not, then, fundamentally, what our parents made or intended, what circumstances have made us, nor what other people think of us. We are not even limited to what we think we are. We are more than we can imagine, because we are made in the image of God, who is by definition beyond our imagination.

Moreover, we are not to be judged, originally or ultimately, by moral performance nor merely by whether we kept or broke certain rules, any more than we are to be judged by our performance at our jobs or even in our homes. From the beginning, we were endowed with certain responsibilities for creation, and later, very important commandments are given, but even these responsibilities do not define who we are *originally*. Who we are is ultimately a gift from God. It is God alone who planned our creation and who made us in God's image. And that plan, that image, is good, a goodness beyond any human standard of judgment, including our own.

What does all this do for people like Sandra and Marlene and Lorne? It means that they can take their feelings of guilt and frustration and failure to God and share them with God. They can go with confidence, knowing that God is present not primarily to judge but to share a concern about what is happening to God's creation, to God's children, to the people made in God's image. It means that they can approach God as cherished persons of great value, who are "good" in God's sight and who therefore can afford to accept themselves for who they are. They do not need to pretend that they have done all they should have done: some of their guilt may be healthy guilt — the guilt of people who know that they, of their own free will, have made wrong choices or taken wrong attitudes. But their guilt does not define them nor need it paralyze them.

---

[14]Ibid., p. 48.

Most of all, they cannot say that they are nobodies, or people of no worth. By definition, by origin, that is simply not true. By going back to their true origins, they can transcend their more recent origins, their parents, their friends, their circumstances. That does not mean they ignore these more recent origins, but they can put them in perspective, assess them and use them as they see fit.

### The Roots of Identity

What going back to our ultimate origins can do for our sense of self-worth was demonstrated to me some years ago. While in New York City, I noticed that Alex Haley was speaking at Barnard College. His talk was fascinating. Haley told the story that he later wrote in *Roots*. He related how, as a boy, he heard his grandmother speak about *her* grandparents, and *their* grandparents, Haley's great-great-great-great-great grandfather, who had been brought to America from Africa as a slave. His slave owners had given him the name of "Toby," but he used to tell his grandchildren, "My name is not Toby; my name is Kunta Kinte," and he would tell them a few words from his native language. Much intrigued by this story, Haley decided as an adult to try and trace his ancestor's place of origin. After incredible research, he set out for Africa to look for the village from which his forebear had come. Once there, he asked the village historian to recite the history of the community. Beginning at the beginning, the historian went through events of note over the years. Eventually he came to the time when a certain "Kunta Kinte" went out one day to cut wood and did not return. He was abducted by slave traders and presumably taken to America. During this long recitation, Haley also learned a great deal about his people's centuries-old customs and culture, developed long before Africa was "discovered" by white people.

It took Haley about ninety minutes, speaking rapidly, to tell his story. While the account itself was engrossing, the effect on the audience, which was about three-quarters black, was even more remarkable. As Haley told about his discovery of his ancestor's home village, its customs, culture and people, the audience became more and more excited. They began to cry out, "Black is beautiful! Black is beautiful!" Then they began to sing that old gospel hymn, "I've wandered far away from God, Now I'm coming home."

At first I wondered why they were singing that hymn, but then it struck me. These people were discovering and celebrating their roots. They had been told, all these years, that they were descended from slaves. Now they had surpassed that origin. Now they recognized more deeply that they were not what people had told them they were, not what they had thought themselves to be. They had an identity independent of what had happened to them in recent history. They now had a perspective from which they could assess what others said about them or what they had said about themselves.

A similar thing happened to many of the people in the Renewal of Faith classes, who heard again the story of our beginnings as told in Genesis. They became excited as they realized that this story was *their* story. The story was not about some other people who lived long ago and far away. It was not just an interesting fable. It was talking about them! They were asked to go home and write their own stories of creation. In doing so, they looked not only for events that had happened to them but also for occasions when they had shaped some order out of chaos, brought some light out of darkness, brought life out of something that seemed lifeless. They were encouraged to say, "That was good."

## Daring to Believe

Of course, making this connection demands a leap of faith. To believe what Genesis says about us and our beginnings and our nature and value is to take on faith a statement that we cannot prove, at least not scientifically. It means believing in the original meaning of *belief*. It means to *love* this story about ourselves. It means to set our hearts on it, to commit ourselves to it, to risk living by it.

This faith is not blind. Something in it strikes a responsive chord, as Haley's story struck the hearts of his black listeners. Something in us is not satisfied to believe that we are nothing but guilty failures. Even when Lapham's friend explodes: "I'm nobody!" his very anger is proof that he ought not to be nobody. He was meant to be somebody, somebody "good." Sandra's decision to seek out some kind of faith was not merely a return to childhood; it was a hearkening to something within her that said she was not a failure. Eleanor's questioning of her employers' goals for her was a response to an inner voice that said: "There is a higher, better purpose and goal for you." And Michael's very presence at the group was really a cry of the heart that said: "There must be more in store for me than this. I must have been meant for something better."

This "inner voice," no matter what we call it, does not rule out all other voices. It is a transcendent voice that helps us to recognize which voices are authentic and which are not.

The story of Lorne, the Native Indian, bears out the power of this voice. For years he wandered in the wilderness, going from job to job, from drunkenness to sobriety and back again, all the while seeking, seeking. Finally he went, by invitation, to a sweat lodge gathering. In that deep, traditional experience he sweated out his own guilt and failure and emerged feeling cleansed and remade. He still had times when he lapsed into his old patterns, but he had a vision of a new kind of self to which he returned. He learned to accept himself as an Indian, as an alcoholic and as just plain Lorne. Somehow he knew that the "voice" in the sweat lodge was the true voice, and it helped him to find and accept his true self.

Bob has somehow found the grace to believe in himself despite rejection by his mother and his church. He cannot understand why God keeps calling him and then setting up roadblocks, but something in him says, "Keep honoring the call and waiting for a way to respond."

When her husband abandoned her, Marlene was left physically and spiritually destitute. But friends asked her to help out as a volunteer and then as a cook in a school. She was terrified at first, but she risked believing them and went on to become a counselor in a center for handicapped people. She found the strength to reject her mother's judgment that her child's handicaps were God's punishment. She found other voices that told her otherwise and that were affirmed by something very deep inside. She dared to believe them.

All these people remind us of the story of Genesis, the story of our beginnings as human beings, the story the authors dared to believe and dared to write in order to inspire our belief. The story of our origins strikes a note of celebration in our hearts and makes us want to join with the sun, moon and stars and all of God's creation in one great paean of joy as we sing:

The spacious firmament on high,
with all the blue ethereal sky,
and spangled heavens, a shining frame,
their great Original proclaim.

The unwearied sun from day to day
does his Creator's power display,
and publishes to every land
the work of an almighty hand.

Soon as the evening shades prevail,
the moon takes up the wondrous tale,
and nightly to the listening earth
repeats the story of her birth,

while all the stars that round her burn,
and all the planets in their turn
confirm the tidings, as they roll,
and spread the truth from pole to pole.

What though in solemn silence all
move round the dark terrestrial ball,
what though no real voice, nor sound,
amidst their radiant orbs be found;

in reason's ear they all rejoice,
and utter forth a glorious voice,
forever singing, as they shine,
*"The hand that made us is divine."*

(Joseph Addison 1672–1719. Emphasis added.
Set to music in Haydn's oratorio, "The Creation.")

# 2

*persons / things*

# *How does our culture value us?*

I T IS EXCITING to discover that we are made in the image of
God. It means that in the eyes of God we are "good" — valued — from the moment of our birth. This goodness is a gift, not
an honor we earn. We are endowed with creativity and imagination and are intended by God to share in the work of caring for
creation and in the ongoing creation of the world. With such a
breathtaking gift and challenge presented to us, why do we not
immediately accept it and rejoice in it?

The gifts of creativity and imagination involve freedom of
choice, and with freedom of choice always comes the possibility
of making mistakes. We are tempted to choose wrongly, or at least
to choose the right for the wrong reasons. It is especially tempting to choose goals that are good and true and even "godlike" but
then to seek ways of achieving them without too much effort.

It is this temptation that the advertising industry of our age
particularly exploits. We receive so much "direct mail" that most
of us simply throw it out. But both the volume and the content
do reveal much about our society and its values. Today I received
a glossy envelope. On the outside it says: "If you have a bold
mind and an adventurous spirit...this invitation is for you." On
the inside it says: "Come see. Come discover. Come be dazzled.
Science is the greatest human adventure of our time, and you're
invited to share it now."

But am I able to comprehend such great scientific adventures?
The ad reassures me. "Of all the people who'll receive this in-

vitation, only a very special group will accept.... If the list from which I got your name is any indication, *you are one of them.*"

But how will I share in such startling discoveries? By subscribing to a special kind of science magazine. In the pages of this magazine I will travel to famous scientific laboratories, "where physicists hope to uncover, within the atom itself, the very forces that created our universe. ('I think,' opines one researcher, 'we may be on the threshold of finding God!')." Surely such an exceptional magazine, designed only for the elite, will be very costly. Not at all. In fact, they will send me the first copy free of charge.

### Garden of Temptation

We are all familiar with this kind of advertisement, so typical of our age. But there is really nothing new about it. In fact, very soon after the lofty stories of creation as told in Genesis — the stories that tell us we are made in the image of God and invited to share in the care and ongoing life of creation — we come to the story of humankind's first temptation:

> Now the serpent was more crafty than any other wild animal that the Lord God had made. He said to the woman, "Did God say, 'You shall not eat from any tree in the garden'?"
>
> The woman said to the serpent, "We may eat of the fruit of the trees in the garden; but God said, 'You shall not eat of the fruit of the tree that is in the middle of the garden, nor shall you touch it, or you shall die.'"
>
> But the serpent said to the woman, "You will not die; for God knows that when you eat of it your eyes will be opened, and you will be like God, knowing good and evil."
>
> So when the woman saw that the tree was good for food, and that it was a delight to the eyes, and that the tree was to be desired to make one wise, she took of its fruit and ate; and she also gave some to her husband, who was with her, and he ate.
>
> Then the eyes of both were opened, and they knew that they were naked; and they sewed fig leaves together and made loincloths for themselves (Genesis 3:1–7).

Does this story not sound suspiciously like the advertisement I received in the mail? The serpent is on the side of the man

and the woman — he wants the best for them. They have been
laboring under the impression that certain things are not for them,
like the fruit of the tree in the middle of the garden. They have
accepted limitations on their knowledge and abilities that are not
supported by facts. They are invited by the serpent to throw off
those limitations and to embrace their full potential — a limitless
potential. They are invited to be gods themselves, with all the
knowledge godhood implies.

And how will this knowledge be acquired? Surely gaining such
knowledge would demand every ounce of ability they had. But
no. It can be had simply by reaching out and eating the fruit of
the tree of the knowledge of good and evil. No cost is involved.
And the fruit comes so highly recommended by one who seems
himself to be so wise. Why not?

Like the serpent, the advertisers offer us things that seem, in
themselves, so right, so good — things we ought to have, things
we have a right to have.

Here is a full-page ad picturing an exclusive perfume that
may be bought at Bloomingdales. "Sumptuous, Sensuous, Seductive" — like the fruit on the tree of knowledge — and it promises
to make me sensuous and seductive. How? By applying this
perfume.

Here is a picture of a red sports car. It is called a "Z" car.
"Pure power," the text says. "Power. That's what a Z-car is
all about. ... You'll call it sleek. Slippery. Sensuous. It turns you
on even before you turn it on. ... It's a driver's car. For the
driver who understands shape. Demands performance. Respects
power ... Pure Z. Your Z. Awesome." And how can I make power
my own, become powerful? Simply by buying and driving the
Z-car.

On another page I see a beautiful, lush green meadow, with a
deep blue sky and fleecy white clouds above it. Against the sky
is the symbol for "pure virgin wool." Seated in the meadow is
a beautiful young woman. Her eyes are clear and earnest. Her
complexion is completely without blemish or wrinkle. She wears
a full-length wool coat, woven in warm earth tones, and on her
lap she holds a sheep, which she also covers with the wool coat.
The caption is, "Pull the Wool Over."

Do I want purity? Do I want to be pure? Of course I do. And
how do I get such purity? By buying, and wearing, pure virgin

wool. Another form of "eating the fruit" of the tree that promises me wisdom.

## Enticing Promises

The spirit of the serpent in the Garden of Eden is alive and well and living in the Western culture of the 1990s. "The serpent" is even more effective on television than in magazines. Western television ads create markets for our products by arousing desires our products are designed to satisfy. They expose, promote and export our values.

The advertisers know and understand our wants very well indeed. They know that we need joy and celebration in our life. They know we want excitement and stimulation, both bodily and intellectually. They know we value power and the feeling that we have power over our lives. They know our need to feel special, unique — not just run-of-the-mill persons. They know we value purity of mind and body. They know we need relaxation and companionship and loving relationships. They know we are not satisfied to remain as we are, that we have aspirations. They appeal to those aspirations, just as the serpent appealed to the aspirations of the man and the woman in the garden.

Most of these aspirations have the ring of integrity about them, although all may be corrupted. All are a part of being truly human. But how are they to be achieved? According to advertising, from the outside: by wearing this or drinking that, by traveling here or flying there, by driving this or acquiring that. Advertisers see us not as individual human beings in whom they are genuinely interested but as customers and consumers of their products. They promise that we can fulfill our aspirations by acquiring what they have to sell.

But if the active ingredient in changing or being fulfilled comes from the outside, then it is not something that we create or work out or work through or agonize over. It is not what evolves as we wrestle with ourselves and with God in the long night watches. It is not knowledge we learn by trial and error and hard choices over a lifetime. It is instant, automatic, and it is "applied," like lotion, to the *exterior* of our lives. But it purports to transform our *inner* beings. If exterior applications could indeed so change us, then we would surely not be human beings made in the image of God, endowed with creative and imaginative powers, but only lifeless objects, much like the products we are urged to buy.

The products and services that various firms may supply are not necessarily useless or harmful. But they cannot fulfill or transform our inner beings nor satisfy our lofty aspirations, the ones inspired by God, those which establish the image of God in us.

The serpent in the garden is not portrayed as evil in himself. He was subtle, clever, crafty, but not necessarily bad. He promised what he could not deliver. He deceived the woman and the man, perhaps, but they were responsible for yielding to the deception, for wanting to be gods, rather than godly. They "bought" his message because they thought it easier to fulfill their aspirations by merely eating a fruit than by a lifetime of working with God in the never-ending pursuit of wisdom.

## Abdicating Personhood

The results were tragic. I am not speaking, in the first place, of the "punishments" described in Genesis 3:14–19: the pain the woman would have in childbirth and her subjection to her husband; the transformation of work for the man into a curse and constant disappointment. I am talking about the experience of nakedness. The man and the woman were naked when first they met, but they were not ashamed. Nakedness as a state in which we are born is but a symbol of our acceptance by God in our original, "natural" condition. But if we discover that we are naked after having pretended to clothe ourselves with wisdom, we may well feel shame and embarrassment.

With our new nakedness comes our uneasiness in the presence of God. Before their ill-fated attempt to acquire divine wisdom by simplistic methods, the newly created humans were in complete harmony with God. They walked with God in the garden in the cool of the day. Perhaps they talked with God about plans for the garden and delighted in its beauty and fruits. They were co-workers in a joint, creative task. Now that they had tried to be independent, to be gods in their own right, the harmony was gone. They had their own agenda, made without reference to God. It had failed and they did not feel free to share their disappointment with God.

It was not enough for them to blame others. When the woman blamed the serpent and the man blamed his wife and even God,

*[Handwritten at top: when we bucked our parents' discipline we were not denying personhood — we were declaring our personhood. individuality (right or wrong)]*

God did not accept their excuses. True, the serpent was held responsible for trying to deceive them, but if God had held the serpent totally responsible, God would have accepted the idea that the human beings were, after all, objects, not persons. In holding them responsible, God was holding to the original concept of human beings as creatures gifted with both the freedom and the responsibility for working out, with their Creator, what kind of beings they would become. The sin was not so much in eating forbidden fruit as in denying personhood, the image of God in them. Their sin allowed them to be defined as things, rather than as persons. *[Handwritten: Were They denying personhood?]*

Similarly, we cannot blame advertisers for our obsession with consumer products. Advertisers have their own guilt to bear, but if we merely blame them, we, like those who blamed the serpent, will have abdicated our role as responsible human beings. We will have ceased being subjects and become objects of life's events and advertisers' imaginations. We will have allowed ourselves to be manipulated rather than to be responsible for our actions.

This, in fact, can happen without a conscious decision. Manipulation attacks the vital domain of the imagination. Imagination, "thinking God's thoughts after God," most fully expresses the image of God in us. The serpent's genius was to tempt the man and the woman to give up imagination in favor of fancy. The serpent urged them to exchange imagining great things with God for fancying a carefree independence for themselves.

*[Handwritten: Imagination is not always thinking God's thoughts. One can imagine evil things as well. Definition]*

### Fanciful Myths

To substitute fancy for imagination trivializes the imagination and demeans the person. The *Funk & Wagnall's Dictionary* (1956) defines *imagination* as "the picturing power or act of the mind; the constructive or creative faculty." It defines *fancy* as "the power or act of forming pleasing, graceful, whimsical, or odd mental images, or of combining this with little regard to rational processes of construction; *imagination in its lower form;* . . . fantasy" (emphasis added). *[Handwritten: but still imagination, high or low]*

It goes on to compare *fancy* and *imagination* in more detail:

Both [*fancy* and *imagination*] recombine and modify mental images; the one great distinction between them is that "fancy" is superficial, while "imagination" is deep, essential, spiritual (emphasis added).

The grave error of the first humans was in *fancying* that they could become like gods instead of *imagining* what it might be like to be godly. Is this our error also? Imagination produces images and images blend into myths. Myths are stories that give us a view of the world and of the people who live in it. When imagination is supplanted by fancy, the myths that are produced are bound to be perverted also. As William Fore expresses it, the myths created by the media and by the advertising world often stand in sharp contrast to the myths of the Bible. We need to be conscious of the great gulf between these myths and of the tensions this gulf rightly creates.[1]

One myth our culture creates is that our deep needs and high aspirations can be satisfied quickly and easily by some product or technique — just what the serpent promised in the garden. This myth also promises quick cures for serious disorders. A flagrant example is the alarming increase in the use of drugs. Cocaine in various forms seems to be most popular right now. The death rate from cocaine use in Ontario rose ten times in three years. In Detroit half the homicides and a third of the suicides were cocaine related.

It seems clear that most people who use drugs do so to escape difficult, painful or stressful situations. It is not surprising to find drug use high among unemployed young people. *Newsweek* magazine reports that in Shaw, a predominantly black neighborhood in Washington, D.C., the average real wages for black men dropped 50 percent in recent years and that about one-third of the men in the area are arrested on drug charges by the time they reach thirty.[2]

But the problem of drugs is obviously not limited to poor black youths. White rock stars, the wealthy and persons in high political office are also afflicted. Many people of all races and from a wide variety of social and economic levels turn to drugs. They have run out of emotional and spiritual resources with which to cope with life's pressures. UCLA criminologist James Q. Wilson says

---

[1]William Fore, *Mythmakers: Gospel, Culture and the Media* (New York: Friendship Press, 1990), pp. 3f.
[2]Larry Martz, "A Dirty Drug Secret," *Newsweek*, February 9, 1990.

## LAWRENCE MEMORIAL LIBRARY

40 North St.
Bristol, VT 05443
453-2366

Hours:

| | |
|---|---|
| Sunday | closed |
| Monday | 1 – 5 |
| Tuesday | 10 – 8 |
| Wednesday | 1 – 8 |
| Thursday | 10 – 8 |
| Friday | 1 – 5 |
| Saturday | ~~1 – 5~~ 9 – 1 |

Preschool Storytime
        Thursday at 10:00

**Bookmarks Courtesy of
Deerleap Books**

get
A window Toward
Heaven by Diane Komp

"Joshua" by

that "cocaine is unlike other drugs: tobacco may shorten life but cocaine debases it. The user feels talkative, affable, brilliant and confident, no matter how far along the slippery slope he or she may be. In reality, however, the high becomes the main goal in life, and the user will rationalize doing almost anything to get the drug." Drug users imagine that they are in control when, in fact, they have lost control. Like the serpent, drugs promise what they cannot deliver.[3]

It is easy to understand why some people in unbearable situations may turn to drugs in desperation. But what may be even more alarming is the addiction to consumerism to which so much of the world has turned. This addiction is strongest in the industrialized countries, but colonialism has exported it to some of the poorer countries while those under communism seem all too eager to embrace it.

### Consumer Capitalism

The most glaring recent example is the revolution taking place in Eastern Europe and in the Soviet Union. Some people in capitalist countries are celebrating this revolution as the triumph of capitalism over communism. But it may well be a much simpler, much more sinister phenomenon. Coleman Romalis, who teaches political science at Toronto's York University, says:

Nothing so inflames the imagination [fancy?] of people everywhere in today's world, [as] the power to buy. The magnetic attraction of blue jeans, dutifully reported by two generations of travelers to the Soviet Union, testifies to the potency of consumer symbols on both sides of the Iron Curtain.

What we are seeing now in Eastern Europe is not so much the triumph of capitalism, as the unstoppable power of advertising. Seventy years of Marxist alternative symbolism since the 1917 Revolution, countless volumes exploring the "fetishism of commodities," have proved no match for the inexorable incursions of the Western advertising industry....
We don't know yet what form the Eastern European countries will take when the power shakeout is finished. What

---

[3]Ibid.

we can forecast, with some certainty, is that the big win-
ners will be Western enterprise, and particularly their main
instrument: the advertising industry.[4]

Capitalism, like the serpent, says: "Surely you want a world
where all have a chance to succeed, to reap the fruits of their
labors and to enjoy the good things of life? Then set the market free and let all compete freely. Those who deserve to win
will win. Those who deserve to lose will lose. Surely that's only
simple justice."

But justice is not done. Wealth begets wealth and poverty
begets poverty. The scales are heavily weighted on the side of the
privileged. Worst of all is the fact that human beings are not content just to reap the rewards of their labors. They want more and
more; they want to be like gods, to have everything. In the process, wholesome incentive and praiseworthy effort are perverted
into greed.

But those who were promised fulfillment by eating the fruit of
competition find that, at the end of the day, they too are naked.
Even capitalism's most ardent defenders, those who have profited
most by it, concede that the system has been corrupted by greed.
People may have acquired a lot, may even feel fulfilled in some
sense. But they can hardly be entirely blind to the ways their
wealth has left others poor. And in their inner selves they, like our
forebears, are not very comfortable when God calls out, "Where
are you?"

U.S. economic historian Robert Heilbroner says:

Capitalism does wonders for economic growth but little
for moral growth or cultural enrichment. Capitalism is a
system full of self-debasement. Witness the commercial vul-
garity that pervades our media-hypnotized culture; it is an
offence to the human spirit. While capitalism's internal economic contradictions are not what will destroy it, its internal
cultural contradiction may.[5]

Indeed, some uneasy champions of capitalism have misgivings
about the system. While they believe that free enterprise is the

---

[4]*Toronto Globe and Mail*, February 23, 1990.
[5]Quoted by Jack Cahill in "Dark Victory," *Toronto Star*, December 17, 1989.

best system yet devised for creating wealth, they find the excesses of greed and the outrageous overconsumption morally repugnant.

## The Choice of the Garden

Unfortunately, such signs of moral repugnance are scarce as yet. For the most part, capitalism continues to treat people like things. Its employees are termed "the labor market." Corporations tend to go where they can pay the lowest wages, regardless of the effects on the people they hire or fire. They continue to buy up companies, as a business leader says, "like pots of jam, firing half the people, then selling [them] again for a profit." Irving Kristol, whom Cahill describes as "a thoughtful capitalist," publishes the conservative U.S. journal the *National Interest*. He summed up the triumph of capitalism over communism this way: "We may have won the Cold War, which is nice — it's more than nice, it's wonderful. But this means that now the enemy is us, not them."[6]

We see now that we have learned how to produce a wide variety of things. Many of us have acquired many things. We are judged by how many things we can acquire or consume. And in the end we have become things. The person has been hidden or lost. And this condition has not been thrust upon us by someone or something else. Sad to say, we have chosen it for ourselves.

These perceptions may sound like a litany of despair for the human race. But they need not be. Remember from Genesis that while God holds the man and the woman responsible for what they have done and drives them out of the garden, God goes with them. God stays with them. God does not condemn them for their sense of shame but helps sew tunics to cover their nakedness. God is still their God and still regards them as children of God, made in God's image. To God, they are still, and always will be, persons, not things.

The Genesis story shows us not what happened to one pair of human beings long ago but what happens to human beings in all ages. All of us have the choice of the two in the garden. Will we accept the gracious gift of being made in God's image with all the privileges and responsibilities that go with that image, or will we try to achieve spiritual goals through things we possess or consume and thus lose our own identities?

---

[6] Ibid.

## Testing

Even Jesus was not spared this test. That is what the story of
the temptations is all about. Jesus uniquely bears the image of
God. That image is confirmed at Jesus' baptism when a voice
from heaven is heard: "You are my Son, the Beloved; with you I
am well pleased" (Mark 1:11). His identity as a child of God is
reaffirmed.

But immediately Jesus is tested. He is tempted to demonstrate
his identity by acts of power: turn stones into bread, rule the
world, save yourself from death by a miracle. Would not such
acts of great power prove that he was indeed a child of God?

But, unlike the first children of God, Jesus did not heed that
temptation. He perceived that being "godly" involved more than
asserting power over the world or performing miracles. The world
might be impressed by such signs, but the true tests of godliness
lay elsewhere. Jesus chose the longer, harder way. But on that way
he learned what it meant to bear the image of God. As the writer
of the letter to the Hebrews puts it: "Although he was a Son [of
God], he learned obedience through what he suffered" (Hebrews
5:8). The purpose of this "education" is clear: "Because he himself
was tested by what he suffered, he is able to help those who are
being tested" (Hebrews 2:18). Jesus learned what the first human
beings failed to learn: that the road to real wisdom is long and
includes suffering as well as joy. In fact, the joy and the suffering
are inseparable parts of realizing that we are children of God. The
writer to the Hebrews understands this:

> Let us . . . lay aside every weight and the sin that clings so
> closely, and let us run with perseverance the race that is
> set before us, looking to Jesus the pioneer and perfecter of
> our faith, who, *for the sake of the joy that was set before him
> endured the cross* . . . (Hebrews 12:1, 2; emphasis added).

Our innermost being attests to this truth. We know from history and experience that true greatness is never handed to a
person on a platter. Everyone, by virtue of the fact that he or she
is made in the image of God, has the potential for true greatness.
But that greatness comes as God's own greatness is understood; it
comes from living through the joys and sorrows of life.

_TRUE TRUE_

All human life has periods of testing. The Hebrew people were delivered from their slavery in Egypt. But they did not arrive at the Promised Land the next day — they wandered for many years in the wilderness. But their wandering was not aimless. Forty years was the time it took to become a people. And it was during those years that on the lonely, bleak top of Mount Sinai, Moses received the Ten Commandments as a sign of the people's covenant with God. Those commandments, we may be sure, were not simply "dictated on the spot." They were forged out of many, many years of human experience and learning at the feet of God.

It was in the wilderness, too, that the Hebrews learned what made them unique. It was not their miraculous escape from the hand of Pharaoh, nor the sudden spouting of water from a rock when they were thirsty, nor the unaccountable provision of manna when they were hungry. No. It was the reality that no matter what they did nor where they went, God traveled with them.

Moses' own greatness was shown by his question to God. He asked not merely where the Promised Land was, nor how long it would take to get there, nor what the rewards would be when they arrived. Instead, he asked, But who will go with us? And God replied, I myself will go with you and set your mind at rest. With a great sigh of relief Moses responds, If You do not go with us, do not ask us to go, for how else will we be different from any other people, except by your going with us? Only your presence makes us unique (see Exodus 33:12–16).

## God with Us

"Followers of Moses" have continued to prove this point. We count as great not those people who acquire the most with the least effort or in the shortest time, but those who have a sense of "being on the side of history," of "going with God," or of God "going with them" — of participating with God and humanity in some great endeavor. Their joy and satisfaction is found in that sense of participation.

It is in this participation with God that we know ourselves to be made in God's image. We discover, with humility and excitement, who we really are. We know that it is not in quick and easy achievements that our true worth is known or proved. It is not in acquiring things or fame. It is in being in the company of God. For God does not travel with "things." God walks with persons.

We know that we have forsaken the image of God in which we were originally made. But to be aware of what we have done is the first step toward repentance and re-creation. Our awareness is also a sign that the original image has not been entirely destroyed. "Things" are not aware of being things. Only persons are aware.

We know that we have defiled the garden provided for us. The question now is "Do we dare to believe that if the garden of innocence cannot be recovered, a landscape of hope can be created? Can we journey out into the real world of the noxious weeds of human corruption and the thorny thickets of difficult decisions, believing that the God who walked in the garden with those first human beings in the cool of the evening will also walk with us in the heat of the day?

# 3

*despair* / *hope*

# *How do we value the world we live in?*

THE CITY of Cairo, Egypt, has five huge garbage dumps. Four are operated by the city or by private companies. But one is operated by the people who live in the dump. Each morning the men and boys go out and collect the garbage in donkey carts. Each afternoon the women and girls sort it: paper, food, glass, plastic, metal. The food is fed to the chickens and pigs. The rest is sold.

You can imagine the scene. I visited the dump a few years ago with some friends. Garbage everywhere. Stench. Pitiful shacks for dwellings shared with pigs and chickens. The feet of dead donkeys protrude from a stagnant ditch. Filth. And flies, flies, flies.

In the center of the garbage dump is a building operated by the church. There, people can go to attend literacy classes, to learn a trade, to share in Bible study and family and domestic concerns. The place is called "Aghabi," an Egyptian adaptation of the Greek word *agape*, which means "love."

Love in a garbage dump? In a place so symbolic of poverty, injustice, disease and hopelessness — of all that is wrong with the world? Some of the people who live in the garbage dump were born there and many could die there. It could be regarded as a place of ultimate despair.

Other such symbolic places are found throughout the world. Some in the "developed" world are characterized not by chronic poverty but by other forms of despair. The hospice for people

45

with AIDS where I worked as a volunteer was far from being a garbage dump. Generous and caring people had provided the best equipped hospice I have ever seen. The residents' rooms were their own to furnish as they wished and were truly private. Beautiful rooms were provided where close relatives could stay.

The nursing staff was exceptional, well-trained and very compassionate. The nurse-patient ratio was double that of an ordinary hospital. The staff included counselors and a chaplain as well as massage therapists and other specialists.

Still, not many people wanted to go there. Residents came to wait for death; the average length of stay was three weeks. Many found that despair could overcome all the bright surroundings. Some struggled with guilt as well. I accompanied one resident going to an eye specialist. (People with AIDS often develop eye trouble and some go blind). He had lost most sight in one eye but the doctor had operated on the other. On the first visit the doctor hoped the man would regain 50 percent of his sight. Good news. He was a great reader. But on the second visit the doctor said, after examination: "I'm very sorry, Arthur. The operation was a failure. I'm afraid there is nothing we can do."

On the way home in the taxi Arthur began to weep. "It's a punishment," he said. "God is punishing me for lusting with my eyes." Fortunately, there were people at the hospice who helped Arthur not to give in to his despair. There was, especially, his adopted mother, his own mother's sister who had adopted Arthur at age six when his mother died. Now she had come across the seas to stay with him as long as he lived. Everyone at the hospice felt her presence. She was the embodiment of love and compassion. There could be no despair so long as she was there.

I came to both dread and anticipate my weekly times at the hospice. Life took on its harshest reality in this place. Here were young men the ages of my own two sons, persons of great gifts and sensitivities and promise, all facing death just when life should be in its bloom. Yet there was love there. And faith and hope.

I remember Chris. The first day I visited him I could see that Chris was suffering from a disorder that slowed his mental processes. When I asked a question, the answer was slow in coming. I asked him: "Chris, how are you coping with your condition? Have you found any resources to draw on?" Chris did not know that I was a minister or, for that matter, a person of any faith. But he replied, after a long pause: "I have discovered the power of Christ."

As the weeks passed, Chris grew weaker. The last day I visited him he was hallucinating. He talked gibberish. Then he fell asleep for a few moments. He woke with a start, not knowing at first where he was. When he remembered and recognized me I asked: "Chris, the first day I met you, I asked whether you had found resources to cope with your situation. Are the resources still there?" Again there was a long pause. Then: "Once you have found it, it never goes away." In spite of Chris's tragic death, I will always remember his hope and his faith.

## Out of the Depths

But can we translate that hope into a view of our world? To hope is to value the world, to see value in it even when circumstances seem to indicate that whatever value it may have had is now utterly lost. Our world seems as depressing as that Cairo garbage dump. It seems as hopeless as an AIDS hospice. Does despair not seem the appropriate response to both such situations?

I remember the reaction of one of my friends when we returned from our visit to the garbage dump. He was very, very angry. Because of the language barrier and because our stay was short, we could not get to know the people there as well as I knew the residents in the AIDS hospice. Nevertheless, we could see and sense a very depressing situation. A world, a society, that could permit human beings to live in such destitution and filth, my friend raged, was corrupt to the core and deserved the wrath of God. And we are part of that world. Is there no health in us?

I felt somewhat ashamed that I did not share his anger more deeply, for it was surely born of a deep sense of justice and caring. But as we talked, we saw the futility of mere anger. It would have to lead to something more constructive, more creative, or it would be anger misspent.

But a hope that arose too quickly could trivialize the enormity of the injustice that we had just seen, just as someone too cheerful entering the room of a person with AIDS could be an affront to the depth of that person's sorrow and suffering. How can we find our way from despair to hope, from anger to grace?

If we are to value our world in spite of its garbage dumps and

tragedies like AIDS, we must find a value beyond present circumstances. Anger, to be creative, must be rooted in the belief that
present circumstances are not what God intended in the beginning
and not what God has in mind for the future. Despair is destructive if it implies that things as they are represent things as they
always will be. It implies that circumstances are more powerful
than human beings and, indeed, more powerful even than God.
Or, worse still, it implies that God intended the world to be as it
now is. Such despair actually "values" circumstances more than
humans and, ultimately, more than God. It makes idols of events
and gods of situations. If consumerism makes persons into things,
then despair makes human beings — even God — into victims.

## Avoidance by Optimism

One way of avoiding such utter cynicism is to escape into positive
thinking or into shallow optimism, always trying to put the best
face on the situation. But that way involves, oftentimes, an even
deeper despair when the optimism turns out to be ill-founded —
when things do not, in fact, turn out well. One definition of *optimism* given by the *Concise Oxford Dictionary* is: "Doctrine ... that
the actual world is the best of all possible worlds." Such a doctrine seems almost obscene in the Cairo garbage dump — "the
best of all possible worlds"? And in the room of the person with
AIDS it seems the ultimate in insensitivity. Obviously, optimism is
different from hope. Hope must be grounded much more deeply.

Any real hope must start with reality. In many ways the world
is surely both corrupt and sick. Injustice seems to be growing,
the rich are getting richer and the poor are getting poorer. In
the United States, the standard of living for the poorest one-fifth
of the population fell by 9 percent from 1979 to 1987, despite
a growing economy during the last five years of the period.
Meanwhile, the top one-fifth increased their standard of living by
19 percent. The famous "trickle down" theory is simply not happening. In Canada, the amount of wealth generated has increased
by 50 percent in five years, but one in seven people — including
a million children — live in poverty. Toronto now has more food
banks than McDonald's outlets.

The injustice is even more glaring when seen on a global scale.
The 20 percent of the world's population who live in the industrialized nations consume 80 percent of the world's goods. Yet the

third-world countries[1] actually *export* to first world countries billions of dollars more than they *receive*. Their standard of living is plunging, the numbers of people starving is increasing. [2]

Meantime, the wealthy nations are reducing their aid not only to poorer nations but also to the poor in their own countries. In the Reagan era the U.S. cut spending for the poor; another eleven million people joined the ranks of those living in poverty. Funds for health care, education, food and housing were cut or had to be stretched to provide less help to more people. A new "street society" arose — people forced to wander, beg, look for nonexistent work and live in makeshift shelters. Worst of all was an insidious doctrine preached by some leaders in Britain, the U.S. and Canada that the poor somehow deserved to be poor, that jobs were available for everyone who would only get out and get them. Thus did many avoid any sense of guilt or responsibility for what was happening to their fellow citizens.

## By Retreat Within

Another way to block out harsh avoid realities is to turn inward, to live in a protected world of our own where we do not see the fruits of greed and poverty around us. This tendency may help us understand why the market for luxury automobiles and million-dollar homes grew rapidly in the 1980s while neighborhoods banded together to keep out any form of low-cost housing. Such housing might give shelter to the less affluent but would threaten the "value" of the homes already there.

The NIMBY syndrome — "not in my back yard" — describes all-too-common symptoms of a certain meanness, an unwillingness to share the misfortune or pain of others. Voices advocating the return of the death penalty grew louder in the 1980s; the number of executions in the U.S. increased. Criminal offenders received longer sentences while tolerance for letting anyone out

---

[1]More accurately called the "two-thirds world." The poor nations of Africa, Asia, Latin America, the Caribbean and the Pacific are commonly referred to as the "third world." This portion of the world, however, represents the majority of the world's people, nations and land mass and is by no means "last" in a just world order, as notions of "first," "second" and "third" worlds would imply.

[2]These statistics are provided by Jack Cahill in the *Toronto Star*, December 17, 1989.

[3]Barbara Ehrenreich, *Fear of Falling: The Inner Life of the Middle Class* (New York: Pantheon Books, 1989), p. 190.

on parole declined. Funding for workable programs of rehabilitation was cut as voters approved new loans to build new prisons.
It was hard to find places in people's hearts or communities for
half-way houses that might help prisoners prepare to return to
society. In one large Ontario community the only site that could
be found for a half-way house for teenage offenders was between
a nuclear energy plant and a waste disposal facility.

Such turning inward may be a way of saying that things are
just too difficult or complicated or ugly for us to face — a form of
despair. Optimism and despair can become two sides of the same
coin. If we dare not face reality we must either pretend that it
does not exist (optimism) or shut it out so that we do not see it
(despair).

## By Lashing Out

Yet another way of dealing with harsh reality is to lash out against
it. Frustrated that we cannot remove it, we strike out at whatever,
or whomever, is closest at hand or most vulnerable. Such violence
is as old as the human race, as the story of Cain's murder of Abel
illustrates. But violence is always finding new ways of expression.
It need not be overt; some of the worst violence may cloak itself
in institutions of law and order. The apartheid system in South
Africa is such an example. While appealing to the African National Congress to renounce violence, those who uphold apartheid
have violated human dignity, perverted justice and denied blacks
equality before the law. The system has blinded itself to the obvious wrong of racism by legitimizing violence in state laws. It is
a system based on fear, the fear of the privileged minority to face
the implications of justice for the dispossessed majority. It is yet
another way of escaping harsh reality.

War is another form of violence. It, too, can be an act of frustration, a way of "setting things right," changing a reality we
cannot abide. Saddam Hussein was overwhelmed by debts in-
curred in Iraq's long war with Iran. A large part of the debt
was owed to neighboring Kuwait, a territory he felt rightly belonged to Iraq. Since he could not pay, nor tolerate such a heavy
indebtedness, he "righted" the situation by annexing Kuwait by
military force. The world reacted in horror but Saddam Hussein
was merely following a time honored pattern of "changing" reality
by violent means.

But war is merely violence on an international scale. We are becoming increasingly aware of violence that is committed every day in our own communities. Many children of all classes are abused sexually and/or physically. And in spite of the rise of the women's movement and the slow but steady promotion of women to positions of greater responsibility and higher income, the incidence of battered wives and violence against women shows no signs of lessening. In Montreal a man ran amok and shot fourteen women university students, simply because they were women or because he saw them as "feminists." At the many vigils held for them, people wondered whether such rampages would be possible unless society implicitly supports taking out anger or frustration by battering women.

Some unbelievable acts of violence have been committed by teenagers from "ordinary" middle-class homes. In the town of Mission, British Columbia, three boys psyched themselves up with push-ups, peach brandy and heavy metal music one Sunday night and hacked to death the rest of the family — mother, father and two smaller children. They then stole the mother's car and calmly drove off. There seemed to be no motive.

Unfortunately, such violence is prevalent in our society. As William Fore points out, "People in the U.S. are more prone to violence than are people of any other industrialized nation.... In the last fifty years the rate of rapes in the United States has increased 700 percent, on a per capita basis."[4] In 1985 there were seven handgun murders in England, eight in Canada and 8,915 in the United States.[5]

Because violence has become such a common way of dealing with life's perceived injustices or personal frustrations, it has become a part of many people's value system. That is, violence, like greed, becomes "a good thing," or at least an acceptable thing. It is portrayed as such every day in the media. Families who try to teach other values find their efforts undermined by the insidious influence of TV programs.

But our media not only preach destructive values like violence; they also dilute or trivialize good values. Like the serpent in the garden, our media tend to offer people the easier way. Or they of-

---

[4]William Fore, *Mythmakers: Gospel, Culture and the Media* (New York: Friendship Press, 1990), p. 109.
[5]Statistics from Handgun Control, Inc., Washington, D.C.

fer what they cannot supply. Human beings long to be lifted out
of themselves into something that is above and beyond them and
yet inspires them. We call it transcendence. We express it and experience it in worship through such means as hymns, prayers, the
sacraments with their sacred water, bread and wine, with soaring
architecture and with symbols such as the cross.

But television programming seldom offers us transcendence; it
offers us entertainment. Neil Postman says,

> The main message of the screen itself is a continual prom-
> ise of entertainment. Both the history and the ever-present
> possibilities of the television screen work against the idea
> that introspection or spiritual transcendence is desirable in
> its presence. The television screen wants you to remember
> that its imagery is always available for your amusement and
> pleasure.[6]

Amusement and entertainment have their purposes, as does
fantasy. They can be good fun and the means to re-creation. It
is only when we substitute entertainment for transcendence or
fantasy for imagination that we lose our priorities. We can recognize this loss when we see so much of TV evangelism making
precisely these substitutions. Many of these "religious" programs
are geared to giving people what they want. They are intended
to entertain, else they could not build an audience and gain the
financial support needed to stay on the air.

If our society is in fact so corrupt, if it is so unjust, so selfish,
so violent, if it has so trivialized the imagination and substituted
entertainment for transcendence, what is our response? The first
reaction is to condemn it wholesale. That way we separate ourselves from it and remain "pure." The second is to allow its
distorted, perverted patterns to shape our values. We become a
part of its distortion. We conform. A third is to be so overwhelmed with the magnitude of the injustice that we cannot
imagine how our values could ever overcome or even cope with
our society. True, some new values are emerging that encourage us: a concern for the environment, movements toward world
peace and equality for women. But some days our faith seems so

[6]Neil Postman, *Amusing Ourselves to Death: Public Discourse in the Age of
Show Business* (New York: Penguin Books, 1986), p. 120.

battered and fragile that we wonder whether it can survive. We despair.

## Chaos Comes Again

Condemnation, conformity and despair — are these the only means to cope with a society that has lost its way? To begin with we might acknowledge that our society is not the first to turn to condemnation, conformity or despair as responses to difficult times. In the Old Testament we find plenty of examples of wholesale condemnations of society. It is almost impossible to count the times God rebukes Judah and Israel for conforming to the cultures around them. As for despair, it runs so deep at times that it seems to have reached God's own self. That helps us to put our own unworthy responses in perspective. But is there no way that we can face reality for what it is yet still maintain our integrity and find hope?

Once more, we find direction in a Genesis story. The writers of Genesis sketch the history of the human race rapidly. Our creation in the image of God moves quickly to the seduction by the serpent. He utters the world's first commercial: "Be fulfilled through consumption." Dire consequences result for human work and relationships.

The saga continues with fearless realism. By the fourth chapter of Genesis, Adam and Eve's younger son has been murdered by his brother (shades of the gruesome family murder in Mission, B.C.). Was violence such a potential human characteristic that it emerged in the second generation? *Interesting thought*

By the sixth chapter of the story of our beginnings, the authors picture God as utterly despairing of the whole human race. So deep has the corruption gone that God can see no solution but to destroy all humankind, indeed the whole of creation, except for one "righteous" man and his family. It appears that God has given up on the world, that God has lost hope, that God, in a sense, has turned to "capital punishment" for all humankind and has even "committed suicide" as a Creator. God is no longer the God who creates but the God who destroys:

> The Lord saw that the wickedness of humankind was great in the earth, and that every inclination [RSV: "imagination"] of the thoughts of their hearts was only evil continually. And

the Lord was sorry that God had made humankind on the earth, and it grieved God to the heart.

So the Lord said, "I will blot out from the earth the human beings I have created — people together with animals and creeping things and birds of the air, for I am sorry that I have made them."

But Noah found favor in the sight of the Lord....Noah was a righteous man, blameless in his generation; Noah walked with God...Now the earth was corrupt in God's sight, and the earth was filled with violence. And God saw that the earth was corrupt; for all flesh had corrupted its ways upon the earth.

And God said to Noah, "I have determined to make an end of all flesh, for the earth is filled with violence because of them; now I am going to destroy them along with the earth. Make yourself an ark of cypress wood; make rooms in the ark, and cover it inside and out with pitch..." (Genesis 6:5–8, 9b, 11–14*).

And the windows of heaven were opened and the rains fell for weeks on end. This was no ordinary flood. Order was giving way to chaos. Creation was being reversed. The "fountains of the earth" were unstopped and water poured up from below. The separation of the waters from the land, which had allowed plants to grow and animal life to be possible, was being dissolved. God's back was turned on God's fundamental and most characteristic act of creation. Now order was banished and chaos reigned again.

### Divine Regret

What terrible acts had humans done that would justify such extreme reaction on God's part? The gory details are not given, the "sins" not enumerated. No, the trouble is more than the sum total of humankind's transgressions. Something much more fundamental has gone wrong. The wording now is more explicit: the earth has become "corrupt." Violence abounds and people's imagination — the wording is powerful — "every imagination of the thoughts of the human heart was only evil continually" (v. 5, adapted). The murder of brother by brother had apparently become common. The seduction of easy wisdom had become typical of the human race. What reason was there for anyone, even God, to hope?

It is the *heart* of humans that is corrupted. In the Hebrew language the heart is the seat of the understanding and the will as well as of the emotions. The heart represents the whole of one's life. And if the human heart has been corrupted, the very image of God is lost. Human beings can apparently no longer even *imagine* what it is like to be created in the image of God.

No wonder it is God's *heart* that is grieved. God does not respond so much in anger as in grief. And in profound regret — regret that God had ever created human beings. What regret could be deeper than believing that one's essential purpose has gone awry? Could God even feel responsible, like a human parent does, for how the children turned out? What greater despair could there be for parents than to regret that they had ever brought children into the world?

But it seems that this regret is followed by a second. As God regretted ever making human beings in the first place, God now regretted that they had been destroyed. A hope glimmers through God's despair. In the very midst of destruction, when all order was being reduced to chaos, "God remembered Noah and all the wild animals and all the domestic animals that were with him in the ark" (8:1). And Noah's first act upon leaving the ark was to offer a sacrifice to God. Could it be that Noah remembered his origins? That he was made in the image of God and meant to walk with God? To recognize the breath of God in his very nostrils?

### God's Courageous Realism

We all know how refreshing it is to run across a real human being just as we have given up on the human race. What alleviated our despair when we visited the garbage dump in Cairo was to find the church center at work there — "Aghabi" — a symbol of love in the midst of so many signs of human callousness. What excited me, in the AIDS hospice, that place of tragic death, was to find faith and compassion and a healing greater than mere curing.

I think finding one righteous person, Noah, was what restored God's confidence in humanity. There was, of course, no guarantee that if a new start were made, things might go better. God has no illusions about the human race, even though it is created in the image of God. *The startling revelation is that God will dare to risk creation even with imperfect, sinful human beings.*

> God's heart says: "I will never again curse the ground because of humankind, for the imagination of the human heart is evil from youth; nor will I ever again destroy every living creature as I have done" (8:21*).

There is a revolution in God's thinking. God will begin the work of creation again, not hoping that human beings will do better the next time, but knowing that the imagination of our hearts is inevitably corrupted. God will take that for granted. This approach is not cynicism; it is realism at its most courageous. It rejects the other options of wholesale condemnation, easy compromise and despair. It is a unique quality of hope.

Genesis gives no indication that God has pared down the plans for creation. God will rebuild with what there is to work with. God will not wait for people to become "good" or worthy. God will take the complex mixture that we call humanity and work with us to continue the task of creation. Human beings are violent, they are greedy, they tend to choose the easy, rather than the hard way. They confuse fancy with imagination and entertainment with transcendence, but God chooses them to be partners anyway.

Perhaps this is not a revolution in God's thinking after all. Perhaps it is just the working out of the original creation. One classic Christian interpretation of creation is that God created the world *ex nihilo*, "out of nothing." Perhaps God did. But Genesis 1 does not dwell on that. Instead it tells about a God who created order *out of chaos* and brought light *out of darkness!* Might we not then also believe that God is able to achieve good results by working even with "evil" people? Or at least with people who have thought of themselves as guilty failures, or let themselves be treated as things rather than persons?

### The Rainbow Reminder

Many scholars believe that the story of creation as found in Genesis 1 was written when the people of Judah were in captivity in Babylon. Their hopes that God would defeat their enemies and lead them back to their beloved Jerusalem showed no signs of being fulfilled. People lost heart. They grew bitter. They were too weak and their captors too strong. When Babylonians asked them to sing one of their native songs they replied bitterly: "How could we sing the Lord's song in a foreign land?" (Psalm 137:4).

But now God was showing the way, the authors of Genesis seem to be saying as they wrote of the Flood. God was not above singing the song of hope nor above making plans for the future of humankind in the very midst of the most discouraging response from the very ones God had created. Why then should captive people not respond by participating in faith with God, without proof of success and in the most discouraging circumstances?

Genesis was not written in a vacuum. It was written in a context and for a purpose. The biblical story of the Flood has many similarities to an old Babylonian story. But the Genesis writers used their story to make an important theological point. In this old story of God's new beginning amid evil circumstances, the writers found the hope their people needed.

But what kind of evidence is given of God's faith in humanity? God strikes a covenant with Noah. In this most unusual covenant, God makes all the promises and asks only that people should trust them. God promises that there will never be another flood, nor any destruction of the earth. As proof, God will re-establish order in the earth:

> As long as the earth endures,
>   seedtime and harvest, cold and heat,
> summer and winter, day and night,
>   shall not cease (8:22).

People may not be trustworthy. People may despair of themselves. They may see no reason to expect that they, or their fellow human beings, can live up to God's plans for them and the earth. But they will be able to overcome their uncertainties because God will provide a reliable framework for them.

God also provides a sign to trust:

God said: "This is the sign of the covenant that I make between me and you and every living creature that is with you, for all future generations: I have set my bow in the clouds, and it shall be a sign of the covenant between me and the

earth. When I bring clouds over the earth and the bow is
seen in the clouds, I will remember my covenant that is between me and you and every living creature of all flesh; and
the waters shall never again become a flood to destroy all
flesh" (9:12–15).

Notice that God sets the rainbow in the clouds to *remind God
of the promise so that God will not forget!*

"When the bow is in the clouds, I will see it and remember the everlasting covenant between God and every living
creature of all flesh that is on the earth" (9:16).

In actuality, "clouds" may well rise again. How will people
know that they do not herald another flood? God will take the
bow usually used to make war and hang it in the clouds as a
sign that destruction will never be God's method again. God's
method will not be punishment or despair but grace and hope. In
their captivity the embittered people had hung their harps on the
willow tree, refusing to play or sing their songs again. They were
assured that God hangs the bow of war in the clouds as a harp
of hope instead of a weapon of despair.

God gave Noah and his family one more evidence of the trust
God placed in them. God knew that they were no angels, that
their imaginations, too, had been perverted, though perhaps less
than others. Noah is called a "righteous" man, but aside from
building the ark his recorded acts and words do not display much
greatness. Yet upon this "ordinary" human being God will build
again. God does not reserve the right to create each new human
being, to make sure each is aware that he or she is made in God's
image. No, God continues to give humans the right to procreate
their own kind. "Be fruitful and multiply and fill the earth," says
God. What confidence! What resolution to work with whatever
forms of humanity may be forthcoming!

## Very Ordinary People

This record of God's remarkable act of faith and humility reminds
us of Jesus, who chose such ordinary people to be his followers.
At times their blindness and lack of imagination frustrated him
almost beyond endurance. He cried out: "You faithless generation,

how much longer must I be among you? How much longer must I put up with you?" (Mark 9:19). Yet in the end, he chose to entrust his message to them, confident that God's Spirit would live in them and work through them also.

Jesus, like God, did not expect perfection of people. On the contrary, he seemed to delight in including in his company people whom "the righteous" excluded for fear of contamination. When he did speak of being "perfect," his term implied "completeness" more than moral purity. He said:

"You have heard that it was said, 'You shall love your neighbor and hate your enemy.' But I say to you, Love your enemies and pray for those who persecute you, so that you may be children of your Father in heaven; for God makes the sun to rise on the evil and on the good, and sends rain on the righteous and on the unrighteous.... Be perfect, therefore, as your heavenly Father is perfect" (Matthew 5:43–45, 48*).

When Jesus calls us to be "perfect," he asks us to include all people, both evil and good, in our compassion and not to exclude them from our friendship.

If the writers of Genesis saw the stories of the creation and the Flood as vehicles of hope for their times, ought we not to do so for our times? God deals with corrupted people and evil situations, it is clear, not with destruction but with the grace of forgiveness and the courage of faith. In God's likeness, Jesus pinned his hopes for God's Kingdom on very ordinary people, though his death on a cross seemed to signal a defeat for the forces of goodness and love.

People who have believed in God and become followers of Jesus down through the ages have dared to believe that God could work with them, imperfect and compromised though they were, toward the goal of the Kingdom. They dared to believe that the world was worth saving, even worth dying for. They saw beauty where others saw only frustration and grief. It was not positive thinking but a way of looking at people and the world through the eyes of God.

The great painter Vincent van Gogh is an example of one who saw the world this way. He said that to believe in God was to

believe that God is "not dead or stuffed, but alive, urging us to
love, with irresistible force...our aim is walking with God." The
expression "walking with God" is significant for our discussion
because Noah was one of the few persons in the Old Testament
of whom it was said: "[He] walked with God" (Genesis 6:9). For
Noah, walking with God seemed to imply that he was close to
God and shared in God's thoughts and plans. For Van Gogh,
walking with God seemed to mean something similar: seeing the
world in ways that others did not see and painting what he saw.
For van Gogh, that involved relying on "ordinary" people, victims
of injustice and suffering, as subjects for his lifelong work.

One of his most famous paintings depicts an old man, seated
by a fire, his head buried in his hands. His fists are clenched
against a face hidden in utter frustration; he appears to be engulfed in grief, a picture of total despair. But the title of the
painting is one of hope: *At Eternity's Gate*. Van Gogh himself
experienced long periods of depression; this particular work was
one he labored over while in an asylum. As one art critic said:
"Even in his deepest moments of sorrow and pain, van Gogh
clung to faith in God and eternity, which he tried to express in
his work."[7] And like the people who worked in Cairo's garbage
dump, van Gogh found God among those society had overlooked
or discounted.

### The Face of God

Van Gogh believed in a living God who urges us "to love, with
irresistible force." Such a love is able to be creative even, or especially, under the most discouraging circumstances. In every age
there are at least a few who catch this vision. One such person in
our age was the famous Ugandan singer/songwriter Philly Bon-
goley Lutaaya. At age thirty-eight, Lutaaya had spent four years
in Sweden as a political refugee. In 1988, twenty years of ethno-
cidal civil war in Uganda had ended and he could safely return.
He had written "Born in Africa," a song expressing the new spirit
of reconciliation, which became the country's unofficial national
anthem. Lutaaya returned not to enjoy his popularity but to announce: "I have AIDS." People were stunned. Many said it was
a publicity stunt to promote his records. At least ten thousand

---

[7]Kathleen Powers Erickson, *Christian Century*, March 21–28, 1990.

people in Uganda have AIDS and an estimated one million men and women, out of a population of sixteen million, are thought to be infected with the HIV virus. But nobody talked about it. Lutaaya decided to devote the rest of his life to breaking down the fear and guilt associated with the disease and to bring hope and acceptance to those who suffered with it.

At first he received little support from the government, the church or society. But undaunted, Lutaaya traveled back and forth across the country, growing weaker and weaker. "Be careful with the way you handle yourselves. We need you!" he begged the young people. One scene in a film about his pilgrimage shows the cathedral in the capital city. The church authorities, after refusing to let Lutaaya sing there, had relented. Lutaaya could have refused to go; they had supported the fear and distrust that aggravated all efforts to deal with the disease openly and courageously. But Lutaaya went. He even composed a song for the occasion; it later became one of the church's hymns.

Philly Lutaaya died in Uganda in December 1989. But his life stands as an example. When his original hopes for himself and his nation were frustrated by AIDS, he did not give way to destructive anger and cynicism. Rather, he used the very tragedy of his own affliction and the hypocrisy, shame and guilt of his people as the setting for his life's vocation. Said film critic Morton Ritts: "His marathon of hope may not have been a cure for AIDS, but 'Born in Africa' suggests it was a powerful antidote to the helplessness and despair that are among the disease's most insidious side-effects."[8]

Helplessness and despair can only be countered by the living values, the dynamic faith, so powerfully illustrated in the Genesis story of God's gracious covenant with humankind after the Flood. God's faith continues to value us and our world even when we have despaired of it and ourselves. God continues to trust us and our future when we have given up. Such trust inspires us to entrust ourselves into the hands of the God who has put a rainbow in the clouds. It dares to trust that any work we may do with God in a world that is often contaminated is not in vain.

The young man who directed the "Aghabi" center in the Cairo garbage dump had begun a promising career in science. We asked

[8]*Broadcast Week Magazine*, March 31–April 6, 1990.

him why he had left it to come to the dump. "Because I love the people here," he replied simply. "They are simple as God is simple. In their face I see the face of God."

What made God decide to abandon the work of destruction and replace it with the work of re-creation? Could it be that, in the midst of the flotsam and jetsam left by the Flood, God saw Noah's face and the faces of the ones who had rejected God? And that in them God saw a reflection of God's own face?

# 4

*individual* / *community*

# *What is the center of our universe?*

I F GOD CALLS US to live in hope rather than in despair, how is that hope expressed? Is it centered in individuals or in communities? Surely it is centered in both, but the emphasis in our society has tended to be on the individual at the expense of the community. Or rather, the emphasis on the individual has diminished not only the community but the individual as well. When individuals are regarded as sufficient unto themselves, they can soon despair of what they aspire to.

I learned this when I built a cottage in a lake district of Ontario. I had never owned a home, and choosing a site, drawing a plan and actually building a place of our very own gave me and my family a great deal of satisfaction. Our cottage was to offer us an escape. There we could do as we pleased without the irritations and responsibilities of urban life. We had our own lake shore, our own place to swim and boat and lie in the sun.

Alas, this Eden did not last. Others discovered it. They built their cottages along the same lake shore. Some were noisy and had late-night parties. Others dumped refuse in the lake. When the usual rains did not fall, the level of our lake was dropped in order to supply the necessary depth for canals through which richer people's yachts traveled in the lakes below ours. Our beach grew weeds. Our docks stood on dry ground. Worst of all, acid rain brought its death-dealing pollution from industries hundreds of miles away.

I found myself going to the local council and crying: "There has to be a law to prevent all this sort of thing!" I found myself speaking to neighbors I had hitherto avoided and saying: "We must get together if we are going to preserve our lake and our way of life here." We needed to form some kind of community. None of us could do it alone. Our very privacy, paradoxically, depended greatly on developing some kind of relationship with one another. We were reaping the fruits of our own selfish individualism. We had to learn the benefits, the absolute necessity, of community.

That community was not only local. The local community might do something about noise, crowding and garbage in our little lake. But the levels of the lakes were controlled by the federal government. And acid rain? Well, that came from across the border and was under the jurisdiction of another federal government. When the two governments tried to work together with the industries involved, the corporations argued that they had to compete in a global market. If environmental restrictions were to be imposed, they should be imposed on a global scale, to be fair to all. And so my wish to sit quietly in my own rustic little cottage on a tiny lake depended on the cooperation of many millions of others.

## Communal Resolve

I was not prepared for this rather obvious truth because I was raised in a society that emphasizes the value and rights of the individual. That emphasis is obviously needed when individuals feel like mere slaves or servants of others. But it can be interpreted too narrowly. Undue stress on the rights and abilities of the individual can lead to a concept of society as a conglomeration of persons thrown together without any relationship or interdependence, a sort of social bag of marbles. In our complex twentieth-century world, we need not only to restore a sense of the moral worth of the individual but to combine it with a sense of the moral worth and strength of the community.[1]

Our Native peoples have much to teach us about the necessity of this balance. A good example of how it can work comes

---

[1]See C.B. MacPherson, *The Political Theory of Possessive Individualism — Hobbes to Locke* (Oxford: Clarendon Press, 1964).

from the Alkali Lake Indian Reserve in British Columbia, Canada. It was, like so many reserves for Native peoples, plagued with alcoholism. The situation seemed hopelessly entrenched. Then one day a teenaged girl, Maggie, announced to her mother: "I'm leaving home. I'm going to live with my grandmother. I can't stand the drinking any longer." Her mother, Clara, was shocked. She vowed to quit drinking.

Then Clara's husband, Cecil, on his way to work one cold morning, met two children on their way to school. They wore only ragged clothing and they were shivering. Cecil asked them: "Have you kids had anything to eat this morning?" "Nothing," they said. That shocked Cecil. Alcohol was depriving their children of food and clothing. He said: "I quit drinking." For months he and Clara were about the only sober people on the reserve.

At Christmas they threw a party. Food was free for anyone who came to the party sober. Only the children came. But that was a beginning. The band council met. The elders met. They decided to join the fight against alcoholism. The elders taught the people the roots of their Native faith. The Roman Catholic and Protestant churches joined in the struggle.

A person arrested for drunkenness was given the option of going to jail or undertaking a period of rehabilitation. When the person chose rehabilitation and had to leave the reserve for a time, people wrote and said: "We believe in you." Individuals went, on behalf of the reserve, to visit the person and to give encouragement. When he or she returned, a job was found, even if only a volunteer job. Within ten years the reserve was 95 percent alcohol free. The community venture became a model that was used on other reserves with similar success.

What happened at the Alkali Lake Reserve shows how a community coped with a situation when it was accepted as everybody's problem, not just a multiplication of individual problems. Fortunately, the Native peoples had a tradition of thinking in terms of the community, of treating all individuals as members of the community. They were able to turn to that tradition to overcome the despair and plight of their members. As long as the condition was looked upon as an individual problem, to be met by individual resources, there was little or no hope.

*Not so, what about the committee work place, clubs etc.*

*?*

## Isolation

Unfortunately, our larger society seems to have no such tradition. We have been taught to be independent individuals, not to be interdependent members of a society or community. In our tradition, we are taught to be self-reliant; one corollary of that teaching is that others must also be self-reliant. Thus we are robbed of any help others might offer us and relieved of any responsibility to help others.

Robert Bellah, a U.S sociologist, along with four colleagues, has devoted an entire book to this concern. In *Habits of the Heart: Individualism and Commitment in American Life*, Bellah quotes Alexis de Tocqueville, a French social philosopher who visited and studied America in the 1830s. Tocqueville observed that Americans emphasized family life, religious tradition and participation in local politics. But he warned against an individualism that might ultimately isolate Americans from one another and thereby undermine the institutions of freedom.[2]

In identifying the roots of individualism, Bellah points to such pioneers a Benjamin Franklin, the ideal poor boy who made good. In his *Poor Richard's Almanack*, Franklin coined such sayings as "God helps those who help themselves," which were supposed to teach people to get along on their own initiative. In this utilitarian individualism, persons were left to themselves and the larger society was left to itself. In its more extreme expressions, such a view held that the very purpose of society was to care for individuals, or to assure that individuals had the freedom to care for themselves. Even the noblest example of the American independent citizen, Abraham Lincoln, as Bellah points out, was remembered as the rail-splitter who went from a log cabin to the White House rather than as the public theologian or the democratic philosopher.

"Independent" individuals, however, usually turn out to be lonely individuals. *Habits of the Heart* quotes one woman as saying: "Many people feel empty and don't know why they feel empty. The reason is we are all social animals and we must live and interact and work together in community to become fulfilled. [But] most people have been sold a bill of goods by our system. I

[2]Robert N. Bellah, Richard Madsen, William M. Sullivan, Ann Swindler and Steven M. Tipton, *Habits of the Heart: Individualism and Commitment in American Life* (New York: Harper & Row, 1985.)

call it the Three C's: cash, convenience, consumerism. It's getting worse. The reason you don't feel a part of it is that nobody is a part of it. Loneliness is a national feeling."[3]

People crave community and so, deprived of a tradition of membership in the larger community, they try to form smaller communities composed of people like themselves. The suburb tried to take the place of the small town but it was only partly "home." People worked in one place and lived in another. Moreover, suburbs lacked the diversity of small towns. The very sameness — of age, marital status, type of occupation, political and cultural attitudes — kept the community relatively shallow. A suburb was still largely a geographical entity in which people tended to live independently of one another. People did not have to learn much about each other nor be open to different opinions.

In modern cities, many people live in apartments deliberately designed to permit isolation. Apartments give people freedom to choose a community that is not defined by location. Residents do not need to get to know the person next door — they can choose people who are like-minded but who live in another part of the city, or they can go to events attended by people like themselves. But again, this seeming multitude of choices can supply only a narrow kind of community that isolates people from having to understand quite different people or to take responsibility for those in entirely different situations. They may see homeless people on the street or know that many have to go to food banks, but they need not actually come into contact with them. They can say: "The homeless or hungry must be 'dependent' types — people whom 'God' didn't help because they did not help themselves." They may give to charities that assist such people, but in so doing they relieve themselves of the opportunity and responsibility of coming face to face with them. They, like those described in the previous chapter, have escaped into themselves.

## Stereotypes and Support

Most of us have lived so long in this kind of limited community that we do not realize how narrow is our outlook nor how undeveloped we are as individual human beings. We don't know what we are missing.

---

[3]Ibid., p. 158.

I recognized these limits when I became a volunteer facilitator with a support group of relatives of people with AIDS. In the first place, I was thrust into a group of people going through terrible agony as they watched their sons or lovers or brothers slowly dying of an incurable disease. Worst of all, they could not speak about it to their neighbors, their friends, at their church or to its pastor, and often not even to other members of their own family. They were alone, tragically alone, at a time when they desperately needed a caring community. So now they came to this group of complete strangers, bonded together only by their pathetic loneliness. I was thrust into a whole new world and I learned more from them than from any group I had ever belonged to.

More than that, I was working in a community different from any I had experienced before. Most of the people with AIDS in our city were homosexual. But now I discovered that most of the volunteer "caregivers" were also gay. One night, at a meeting of the facilitators of the various support groups, I looked at the dozen or so people around the room and realized that I was the only non-gay person present. I got a small taste of what it must be like to be a member of a minority group, especially a minority that, for the most part, had to conceal its identity. By moving out of the confines of my little community of people like myself, I caught a glimpse of a wider human community. In so doing, I saw how easily I had accepted a stereotype of a part of society other than the one to which I belong and had adopted one set of moral and cultural values without questioning them. As a result, both society and I had been the poorer.

Many groups, like the one of which I had become a member, model the concept of community because they are needed to support individuals who are either rejected by society or who are going through trials they cannot share with the community at large. But other groups distort the concept of community when they exist for purely selfish reasons, when they are formed to exploit society for their own benefit.

The free enterprise system often operates this way. Under the guise of championing the freedom of individuals or groups to develop themselves, it often operates primarily to exercise the "freedom" of one group at the expense of the freedom of other groups. Speaking to business leaders on his visit to Mexico, Pope John Paul II warned them against the capitalist system that often leads to "the excessive hoarding of goods by a few [which] keeps them from a majority." Capitalism, he said, contains "the temptation to convert the national community into something at the service of the special interests of the company."[4]

The East European countries are learning some of the pitfalls of the so-called free market system even as they hurry to embrace it. They are painfully aware that the communist system that controlled all aspects of the market has failed. What they did not realize firsthand, however, is that the free market system can be very heartless. The old system guaranteed everyone a job and wages. But some were always "more equal" than others and huge bureaucracies bogged down. Now East Europeans have to face the specter of unemployment. In Poland, for example, the World Bank estimates that a million people will be out of work; an economic adviser to the government estimates that as many as 2.7 million, or 15 percent, will be unemployed. Jan Litynski, the chief adviser of the labor ministry and a founding member of Solidarity, says: "We were like mice who did not know there were cats. Now we discover the cat of unemployment in the real world of the free market."[5] According to one point of view, the threat of unemployment ultimately motivates people to find work. But we know that individual motivation is not, in itself, a solution to unemployment. The free market is often a form of selfish individualism writ large.

### Racism

Individualism can also express itself in society through racism — another consequence of a false sense of community. Basically, racism occurs when one community formed on the basis of race or color binds itself together to "protect" itself, or its interests, against another community.

In West Germany, many jobs given to newly arriving East Germans were created by dismissing *Gässtarbeiter* (guest workers), who are mostly Turks and Yugoslavs. These guest workers were allowed to work in Germany but not to become citizens — to become part of the community. East Germans, meanwhile, automatically became citizens. In several East European countries it was the Vietnamese immigrant workers who were made unwelcome.

---

[4]Quoted in *Catholic New Times*, May 27, 1990.
[5]*Toronto Star*, May 13, 1990.

Meanwhile, anti-Semitism has again reared its ugly head in several areas, notably in the USSR, where the ultranationalist Pamyat movement has become surprisingly active. And the "Soviet Union" is already losing some of its unity as ethnic groups, now able to speak out freely because of *glasnost*, resume their ancient animosities.

In the West, racism is "alive and well" to a discouraging degree. In the United States, built on equality and freedom for all, parts of the country resemble the two-thirds world in terms of poverty, poor health and functional illiteracy. In some communities of "the Delta," an area of 214 counties stretching along the Mississippi River from St. Louis to New Orleans, 29 of every 1,000 babies die before they are a year old. That rate of infant mortality is higher than that of Chile, Cuba, Malaysia or French Guiana. In Sharkey County, Mississippi, 60 percent of the residents are functionally illiterate. The per capita income in the Delta in 1985 averaged $8,224, compared to the national average of $12,464. One in five lives below the poverty line.[6]

It is no coincidence that the Delta's population has a high percentage of blacks. Dr. Ronald Myers, a black physician who has chosen to work in Tchula, Mississippi, says: "Racism is the base reason why the Delta is the way it is today. In the Delta, if you are black, you know exactly where you stand." He has received no help from the white leaders in the community for his newly established health clinic.[7]

Once again we see racism as a form of narrow individualism, where one social group bands together to protect its superior privileges at the expense of others. Or we can see racism as one group turning inward because another group's culture seems strange or foreign. If they risked getting to know these "others," their stereotypes might be shattered and they might start to question their own culture. Or their callous indifference and irresponsible attitude toward others' needs might be challenged.

Most Canadians believe that racism has not been a factor in their society. That illusion could be accepted so long as Canadian society was more or less homogeneous. But now minorities are becoming more numerous and more visible; 40 percent of

---

[6]Bob Hepburn, "Life in the Ethiopia of the U.S.," *Toronto Star*, May 19, 1990.
[7]Bob Hepburn, "Racism New and Old Permeates Delta," *Toronto Star*, May 19, 1990.

Canadians have a first language other than English or French. Latent racism is now becoming apparent, especially in larger cities. A ruling that would allow a Sikh to wear his traditional turban in the Royal Canadian Mounted Police caused a national controversy. Meanwhile, tensions developed between Toronto police and the increasing black community in that city. As a defense lawyer for a police officer who shot and wounded a black teenager explained: "The police, almost all of them white, are scared of the blacks. They know intellectually that not all blacks are crooks, but emotionally, in their gut, it's a different story. . . . Toronto police live almost exclusively in a white world, and they police black neighborhoods like an army of occupation."[8]

Again "community" is being defined in narrow terms. The white community is not in touch with the black community. The two communities fear each other. Weaknesses and dangers result when a community divides according to color or any other limited definition. Such communities, isolated and alienated from one another, prevent a true, larger community from forming.

## The Need to Belong

But perhaps these examples of limited community are not entirely negative. Perhaps they are signs of a deep longing that has to be expressed somehow. We live in rapidly changing times. Many things people once took for granted can no longer be regarded as normal. Most of all, many people do not know where they belong, or whether they belong anywhere. And the need to belong is a fundamental need.

The feeling that we do not belong in the larger picture leads us to protest. Protesters may well band together to form a community in which they do feel they have an identity, even if it is initially only a community of the rejected. In fact, for some people it is only as they feel rejected by the larger community that they discover their membership in the smaller one and cherish it as they never did before.

It would be a mistake to accuse all special groups, be they ethnic, racial, cultural, regional, economic, religious or some other, of being narrow-minded bigots. It would be wrong to say that all are motivated by self-interest only. It may be that only as people

---

[8]*Toronto Globe and Mail*, May 17, 1990.

assert themselves in a small but organized and vocal group can they be heard and acknowledged, thereby claiming membership in the larger community.

Richard Gwyn, a writer on international affairs for the *Toronto Star*, says:

> The new potency of ethnicity is in part a defensive response to the new potency of globalism: People feel the need to reassert the local control they have lost to distant financial and economic forces. The decline in the cohesion of the family unit has to be a factor also. In today's wide, wide world, to be alone is to be very vulnerable. The tribe offers a sense of belonging, a social support system, the comfort of familiarity. Until recently, the word "tribe" was used only as a put-down. This attitude is obsolete. Ethnicity now possesses a potency that we have to come to terms with.[9]

The freedom movements in East Europe are a revolt against the oppression of a regime in which most felt they had no part. The Reform Party that has arisen in Western Canada has an ideology many would reject but it offers a vehicle for members to protest their alienation from Central Canada and affirm their own identity. Everyone wants to belong to a distinct society. Everyone wants to feel unique, and paradoxically perhaps, the only way we can feel unique is by belonging to a group with a special character. Perhaps what we are seeing on the world scene is not so much a break-up of larger communities into smaller ones as rejection of one kind of larger community in which people felt they had little or no part, and insistence on a larger, more inclusive community in which all may have a part by virtue of their own distinctness.

If so, it will be important to distinguish between those groupings that are based mainly on using their united strength to exploit others in order to gain power or wealth for themselves and those groupings that are based on defining and expressing their own individuality. The latter encourage others to do the same about their uniqueness.

Many women experience the structures by which most of our institutions operate — our governments, our businesses, our

---

[9]*Toronto Star*, May 13, 1990.

churches, our schools and universities — as excluding them. They do not feel at home in the male hierarchical domains with their emphasis on power, competition and individual achievement. Many find their identity more in gatherings where power is shared with the group rather than centered in individuals. They want to create organizations that operate on these principles. They need places where they can feel comfortable and express their own spiritual identities. They need groups that can protest society's exclusive patterns and work for more inclusive patterns.

Gay and lesbian people do not want to live in a ghetto for homosexual people, but they do want to have gay social clubs and gay congregations where they can be open about their sexual identity. They need the support of others of the same sexual orientation. They need a place where they feel they belong. Such groups can also challenge heterosexual people to think more seriously about their own sexuality and to embrace it as a part of their own wholeness as persons.

Similarly, many groups have formed in response to the widespread concern for the environment. They are more able than are individuals to effect change. Industries and corporations are rapidly being compelled to see that they can no longer treat nature as a mere commodity. Green parties that campaign on a platform of saving nature from the ravages of unrestrained economic policies are proving a force to be reckoned with.

### Speaking for Wolf

Churches are especially well-equipped to provide a place for people who want to express their identity as spiritual beings.[10] As some aver, especially those who have been disillusioned by organized religion, persons may well approach God directly without belonging to any particular religion and without attending any services of worship. But it is also true — and this is a truth we individualists have often overlooked — that as society becomes more and more secular, with open Sundays reducing the rhythm of life to working and shopping, human beings need times and

---

[10]Here our emphasis is on churches because we are addressing those who in some way claim the biblical, Christian tradition. Synagogues, mosques, temples and other places and ways of gathering for worship, of course, serve similar purposes for other religious traditions.

places to gather with others to recognize that they are souls as well as bodies.

Sometimes our services of worship fail to meet this spiritual need. If so, we should conclude not that regular worship is irrelevant but that the more uniformly secular a society becomes, the more distinctly spiritual worship needs to be. As we have noted, church attendance may be increased by aping secular entertainment patterns, but then churches merely become alternate places of amusement. What is essential is that worship allow us to recognize that we are gathered to celebrate our unique nature as spiritual beings. In so doing we do not cut ourselves off from the secular world but minister to it by reminding it of an essential dimension it has neglected. In this way the church can be a model to the world of a more complete community.

The church can also offer the world a vision of a community that encompasses yet extends far beyond human beings. It can offer a different view of nature. The Genesis account of creation makes it quite clear that human beings are part of nature. The phrase about humans having been given "dominion" over nature (Genesis 1:28) has been interpreted to mean that we can use the environment for our own survival and pleasure. This is not the original intent. We would come closer to the writers' meaning if we said that we were charged by God to be stewards of the environment, responsible for its health and ongoing creative activity. Our origin and destiny are part of nature's origin and destiny.

We can begin by thinking of ourselves as advocates for nature. Insights from Native spirituality can help us here. The Oneida Indians tell an old story about the tribe moving to a new place. The location seemed perfect, but they discovered that many wolves already lived there. What should they do? Slaughter the wolves? But then they thought: "What kind of people would we become if we killed the wolves?" Instead, they decided to appoint one person to attend the council meetings and "speak for wolf." An American environmentalist, who retold this story during a forum on the environment conducted by *Harper's* magazine, concludes that we too must learn to "speak for wolf," to speak for the environment.[11] This statement reminds us of Archbishop

---

[11] *Harper's*, April 1990.

Romero's commitment: "The poor have no voice. I will be their voice."

But speaking as advocates *for* the environment is only a beginning. We also need to "speak *with*" the environment. That is, we need to identify with the environment, just as Archbishop Romero identified with the poor of El Salvador. Christians must join people of other religions in leading the world to care for the environment, not simply out of fear for our survival but out of a faith that we belong to nature. We are already beginning to realize that if we continue to destroy our forests we will destroy ourselves as well.

## A Community of Being

But surely we can act from motives more lofty than the fear of our own annihilation. We can begin by acknowledging that our forebears, including our spiritual ancestors, who "discovered" the Americas, regarded the "new" lands as bounty for their own benefit. The Native peoples were regarded as savages to be exploited, defeated, educated and converted to the "white man's" way of life. The vast expanses of rivers, forests, mountains and prairies they saw as wilderness to be tamed, cleared or mined. They talked about "opening up" the territory, "cultivating" it, "developing" it for their own purposes.

In this relationship nature is the object, and we are the subject. We know what happens between human beings when that attitude prevails. In his book *I and Thou*, Martin Buber pointed out how we destroy relationships when we treat another person as an object, as a thing, as "it." Only when we treat people as persons, when we address them as "thou," is the relationship authentic and fruitful. Now feminist theologians like Linda Holler take this truth one step further. We must develop a relationship of mutuality with nature, they urge. That is, we must acknowledge that nature has its own identity, that it is an end in itself, that it exists not only to serve us. Nature is "thou," not "it."

This means, says Holler, that we do not regard ourselves as the center of the universe, making our domination of nature more important than our own dependence on our Creator. This healthy humility is basic for forming true community: not only does it let nature, and others, be themselves, but it allows us to develop our own beings as individuals. It also allows us to develop true values.

*what a difficult concept but how necessary to develop the concept. Ponder it.*

It sees that values are not based primarily upon how "useful" they are for us. Rather, it envisions an ultimate worth that transcends our individual purposes or needs, a purpose in which we find our place along with other parts of creation.

When we cut ourselves off from the community of varied beings, as we noted earlier, we diminish ourselves. "Our own lives are artificial when we are enclosed within ourselves," says Holler.[12] "Value is not an isolated reality that exists in itself, outside of the encounter among beings." When we extend this valuing to our relationship with nature, a tree does not become a person, but in treating a tree as something of worth, *we* become persons. We create a larger "community of being."

This spiritual approach to nature motivates us not from fear of annihilation nor from guilt over what we have done to nature. Instead we are motivated by hope and by the excitement of creating, with nature, new relationships and a new kind of community. We see ourselves (as Frederick Turner, another member of the Harper's forum put it) "as part of a universe whose drama has just begun." To do so expands our idea of community radically while giving each human being a sense of purpose and value.

## A City Worth Saving?

The Bible repeatedly enlarges our concept of community. Creation begins as the story of nature and humanity, not just of individuals. And, as the story of the Flood shows, God thinks in terms of the salvation or destruction of creation as a whole. The world is all one big, interdependent community.

Inevitably, however, we tend to divide the human community into those who are more worthy and those who are less worthy. In Genesis 18, God and Abraham discuss these lines of separation. God has decided to destroy the city of Sodom because of its wickedness, but Abraham protests such a plan. "Will you indeed sweep away the righteous with the wicked?" he asks. It does not seem to occur to him that God might save the good people and destroy the evil ones. They are all in it together, he assumes. "Suppose there are fifty righteous within the city ... forty-five ... forty ... thirty ... twenty ... even ten ... will you

---

[12]Linda Holler, "Is There a Thou Within Nature? A Dialogue with H. Richard Niebuhr," *Journal of Religious Ethics* 17, no. 1 (Spring 1989).

then sweep away the place and not forgive it for the . . . righteous who are in it? Far be it from you to do such a thing, to slay the righteous with the wicked! . . . Shall not the Judge of all the earth do what is just?" (Genesis 18:16–33 passim). God is persuaded. God will not destroy the city if ten good persons can be found in it.

In the end, Sodom is destroyed. Only Abraham's nephew Lot and his wife and his two daughters are saved. But the point of the story is not that a few righteous individuals were saved, but that there were not enough of them — not even ten — to save the city. Abraham is not concerned that he and his family be saved but that Sodom, wicked though it undoubtedly is, be saved for the sake of the redemptive potential of the righteous few. Sodom, too, is part of God's universal community. The righteous, few though they be, are Sodom's only hope. Has God given up on them too?

Abraham here is a kind of Noah, yet he goes beyond Noah. Like Noah, Abraham is forewarned of God's plans to destroy wickedness. Noah and Abraham are both "righteous" figures on whom a future society might be built. But Noah seems passive. He does not question God's plan; he simply does what God tells him. But Abraham, in fear and trembling, dares to challenge God. He seems to be reminding God that Sodom also belongs to God's creation and that its destruction, though richly deserved, goes against God's care for all creation.

## Leaven for the Whole Loaf

But there is more to his argument. Abraham belongs to a tradition that assumes collective guilt; no part of a community can claim that it bears no responsibility for the community's wrongdoing. But Abraham seems to be insisting that the hope for any community lies in the few righteous people in it. Justice does not simply *reward* the righteous; justice, in the sense of wanting a just society, *needs* the righteous if the community is to be saved from the consequences of its wickedness. If God, therefore, destroys the righteous along with the wicked, the community is indeed doomed.

In Old Testament thought, "the righteous" are not merely people who have obeyed God's commandments. They are people who are in right relationship with God — in communion with God. Similarly, the "righteousness of God" does not refer simply to God's moral perfection but to God's relationship with creation. Abraham challenges God: "Will you destroy part of your creation because of the wickedness of the many, taking the innocent with them? Or will you forgive the wicked many for the sake of the innocent few?" Abraham's question is a challenge to God's graciousness.

Abraham's request also expresses confidence in the way God can use the few to redeem the many. It matches God's promise to give Abraham and Sarah a child when they are far past childbearing age and, through that child, to make them founders of a great nation. This promise is made in the context of the dialogue between Abraham and God over the future of Sodom. If God can create a great nation from parents thought to be beyond having a child, could not Sodom be saved when it is thought to be beyond redemption?

Abraham's argument challenges the way we value both individuals and the community. While God's love is all-embracing, God nevertheless distinguishes clearly between righteousness and wickedness. The actions of individuals are extremely important. But the point of choosing the right is not just to become a better individual. It is to become a partner with God in the work of redeeming society. The redemption of the individual and the redemption of the community are thus closely intertwined.

The concept of the suffering servant in Isaiah 53 takes up this theme and enlarges on it in passages that have become familiar and beloved to both Jews and Christians through the centuries. The servant figure is the innocent one (or community) who suffers on behalf of the larger community.

> The righteous one, my servant, shall make many righteous,
>     and he shall bear their iniquities.
> Therefore I will allot him a portion with the great...,
> because he poured out himself to death,
>     and was numbered with the transgressors;
> yet he bore the sin of many,
>     and made intercession for the transgressors.
>                                         (Isaiah 53:11b–12)

The full impact of this truth comes to a climax in the mission of Jesus himself. He was the truly righteous one. Yet, according to the Gospel of John, God did not send this truly righteous one to put us all to shame for our obvious moral failures. God sent him as a means of saving us from the devastating consequences of our wrong ways. Jesus did not separate himself from us but identified himself with us, thus enabling us to follow his way. As John puts it:

> For God so loved the world that God gave God's only Son, so that everyone who believes in him may not perish but have eternal life. Indeed, God did not send the Son into the world to condemn the world, but in order that the world might be saved through him" (John 3:16–17*).

In calling us as individuals to follow him, Jesus also calls us, as a community of believers, to be a redemptive community. We are called to be the salt of the earth, the light of the world, the transforming leaven in the lump.

## Repenting and Changing

The community we call the Christian church is called to be a special kind of community, a group of believers in Christ. But its very separateness allows it to minister in a special way to the world. As "the Word became flesh and dwelt among us" (John 1:14 KJV) in order to show us God's "heart" (v. 18), so the church dwells in the world in order to show the world the heart of God.

Baptism is an act in which an individual is accepted into this special community. But baptism also implies that this individual will be involved in the community's mission in the world. Similarly, in communion we remember the Christ who said: "This is my body which is broken for you," and are empowered to give our bodies to be broken for the world.

We know that the great evils of our day — poverty, racism, narrow nationalisms, the desecration of the environment — cannot be redeemed by individual action. Effective action to overcome them can be undertaken only by dedicated communities. But as people of faith we are reminded that the individualism so common in our day is not our truest tradition. As we have seen, the biblical tradition is community, community with God and with one another. The biblical passages also remind us that our human tendency to separate people by race and class and gender has not begun with us. It seems to have been there from the origins of human society. Our utilitarian attitude toward nature, though contrary to God's original intention and instruction, is also long entrenched. We are only the latest generation to yield to selfishness and greed.

Looking back helps us understand how deeply ingrained these prejudices and attitudes can be. It helps us understand how our world got this way. It helps us to understand why society, our human community, needs to repent and be changed: that individual repentance is not enough. It would be naive, we know, to think that society is ready for radical repentance of the kind that is needed. As Robert Bellah says: "It is not clear that many Americans are prepared to consider a significant change in the way we have been living. The allure of the packaged good life is still strong, though dissatisfaction is widespread. Americans are fairly ingenious in finding temporary ways to counteract the harsher consequences of our changed social ecology. Livy's words about ancient Rome also apply to us, 'We have reached the point where we cannot bear either our vices or their cure.' "[13]

## A Larger Vision

But we can see signs of hope on the horizon. Other values are at work as well. A deep yearning for something genuinely spiritual fills many who have become disillusioned with the limitations of living unto oneself. Concern for the future of our planet is genuine. Dramatic shifts are under way. Despite setbacks and footdragging in high places, the cold war is ending. We are realizing that we can no longer live in two worlds staring in hostility toward one another, that we will live or die together, that we obviously belong to one human family.

Words of hope are being spoken. Dave Foreman, the founder of an environmental group, calls us to seek a "new covenant with the land." The year 1992, the 500th anniversary of the European discovery of America, could be a symbolic time. There are important actions to be taken. Foreman calls us to apologize to our Native peoples, to announce goals to cut by 50 percent America's consumption of paper, wood, minerals, energy and water by the year 2000.[14] This vision echoes the ancient Hebrew law of the ju-

[13]Bellah et al., *Habits of the Heart*, p. 294.
[14]*Harper's* magazine, April 1990.

bilee year, when all debts are forgiven, all slaves freed, all land restored to the original owners (Leviticus 25). Does it not, in fact, sound like a renunciation of many forms of narrow individualism by which we have lived for centuries and a venture of faith into a community of caring with others and with nature?

Caring is at the center of our faith. There is a kind of caring that can easily become paternalism. But true caring builds community. True caring costs. Before going to the cross, Jesus looked over his beloved city. It would have been tempting to curse it and to abandon it. Instead, he wept over it:

> "Jerusalem, Jerusalem, the city that kills the prophets and stones those who are sent to it! How often have I desired to gather your children together as a hen gathers her brood under her wings, and you were not willing! See, your house is left to you, desolate!" (Matthew 23:37–38).

And then he went out to die for it.

This kind of godlike tenacity inspires the church in this and every age to go beyond all ordinary forms of community. Individuals alone are limited, but persons who catch a vision of the Reign of God as described by Jesus can give leadership in forming new kinds of community needed now.

In February 1990, East Germany was turbulent. Just as people were experiencing their first taste of freedom in over forty years, hatred for former communist masters was exploding. Erich Honecker, the former prime minister, was awaiting trial on charges of high treason. No prison seemed a safe place to keep him, and in the meantime he was weakened by recent surgery. Where could he go? A Protestant pastor in Leipzig, Ulrich Seidel, who had been in the vanguard of the East Germans' popular uprising against the Honecker regime, took Honecker and his wife into his home. People demonstrated outside the pastor's church with banners reading: "Asylum for Communist criminals — we Christians should be ashamed." But the pastor felt no shame. He had a different set of values.[15]

As an individual, Seidel had committed himself to a larger faith than one that reserved Christian compassion for Christians.

---

[15]*Christian Century*, February 28, 1990.

As a citizen who loved his country, he had joined with other concerned people to challenge the tyrannical regime headed by Honecker. But now, as a member of the Christian church he had challenged the limitations of a community that excluded its former enemy, Honecker. He risked his fellow citizens' rejection and wrath because of his commitment to a larger vision and in the hope that he might inspire them to this vision as well. His personal values were offered in the service of God's redeeming love for the world. He reminds us of the suffering servant of Isaiah 53. He is a kind of Christlike figure, weeping over his own city and willing to die for it.

## Redemptive Community

In Korea, a woman minister named Young Kim has helped to form a community called "Women Church of Korea" to help the Korean churches accept women as equals. Young Kim was raised as a Confucian and accepted the belief that women were inferior and subservient to men. Then, while attending Ehwa Women's University in Seoul, Kim was converted to Christianity. She married a minister and later became a minister herself. But she was shocked to see that the inferiority of women was accepted by the Christian church as it had been in her Confucian tradition. She vowed to change that.

Young Kim was inspired by Jesus' parable of the woman and the lost coin (Luke 15:8–10). Like the woman in this story, Kim says, the church must search diligently for "women at every corner living in darkness." As the woman lit a candle to aid in her search, so Kim sees "Women Church" lighting the candle of the church so that it may become "a light shining to all of Christianity as we search by candlelight for women lost in Korean society, women who are God's silver coins."

In turn, Kim sees Korean churches leading Korean society to work for justice, peace and the integrity of creation. She and her companions share this vision as they celebrate an Agape Meal together. They share rice and chilled ginger tea in remembrance of Jesus' eating and drinking with many whom society had demeaned or rejected. As they bring to life Jesus' ancient parable, they come to life themselves as individual Christians and they create a symbol of what true community can mean. Kim's conversion began as an individual change, but it was soon enlarged to form a community of women concerned for a much-needed change in the church's attitude to women. And the community's vision went on to dream of the church, in turn, becoming a community committed to changing Korean society.

In a way more mysterious and wonderful than anyone can fully understand or express, Young Kim and Ulrich Seidel become part of a redemptive community to which Noah and Abraham and Sarah and the suffering servant of Isaiah 53 and Jesus Christ belong. They also belong to the community of which Cecil and Clara of the Alkali Lake Reserve in British Columbia are a part. And all of them challenge and inspire us to join the gathering throng.

We began by asking: "What is the center of our universe: the individual or the community?" Surely, we have said, it ought to be both. But, on second thought, we should say neither. The center of the universe is God. When individuals or communities make themselves the center, they reduce the universe to the limitations of their concerns.

Our values, we have claimed, are what we love, what we are committed to. The summary of the commandments affirmed by Jesus makes it clear that our first love is God: we are to love God with all our hearts. And our second love is our neighbor: we are to love our neighbor as ourselves.[16] "Our neighbor," in light of what we have said about our relationship not only to other people but to nature, includes the whole of God's creation.

Is the ultimate love, the ultimate "value" then, to love everyone and everything? Is this possible for mere human beings? Does it not impose on us an impossible burden as we contemplate all the world's needs? It is to this question that we must now turn.

---

[16]See Luke 10:25–37; Matthew 22:37–40.

# 5

*fragmentation* / *integration*

# How do we choose between so many conflicting values?

T HE MORNING'S MAIL always poses a problem for me. It always brings several appeals for financial contributions — sometimes seven or eight appeals at once. I know that the next morning will bring another batch. I can't give to them all. How can I decide which are the best? My financial resources are limited and I don't have enough time to assess the appeals. Shall I toss them all out? Or draw lots?

It would be a lot easier if some appeals were obviously worthless. But virtually all are valid and good. Several want me to help groups fighting for the survival of our environment. Some are from peace groups, some for self-development projects in the two-thirds world. People in Ethiopia and the Sudan will starve to death because of the drought if I don't give. The United Appeal is an umbrella organization that helps such local causes as shelters for battered women and low-cost housing projects. Appeals arrive from food banks, from public broadcasting, from struggling artistic groups. And of course each educational institution I have attended is trying to meet an expanding budget with shrinking resources. If I don't give, am I saying I don't appreciate what they did for me years ago? And I haven't even mentioned the appeal of my local church and the denomination's Mission and Service Fund for its work in our country and in the world.

But these good appeals for money don't press me as much as the many demands on my time and energy — and on my very "soul." I remember Sandra (chapter 1). She felt torn between the legitimate demands of her job as a counselor with troubled teenagers, the demands of her own teenage children, the stress of being a single parent and her uneasiness about the failure of her marriage. On top of all this she felt she ought to be more involved in the many social causes she so genuinely believed in. And money was a constant anxiety: how to make her modest income stretch over the rising costs of rent, food, clothing and so many unforeseen incidentals.

Some days Sandra was angry — angry with herself for not being able to manage everything, angry with her clients for expecting her to solve all their problems, angry with her children for assuming that she would always be there for them, angry with life for being a series of unending demands. When would she, when would anybody, have time for *her* needs? She felt that life had clawed her into little pieces.

Sandra is experiencing the fragmentation and complexity of our modern era. Some days she wishes she could go back to the kind of life her mother had. Her mother had grown up in a small town where everybody knew everybody and people seemed to care for each other. There was a certain unspoken structure that people fitted into. Marriages seemed more stable. Children were satisfied with fewer material goods. There wasn't so much ambition; people seemed to accept their lot in life.

But then she thought: I have freedoms my mother never had. I have been able to go to university, to choose a career, to establish an identity and not just be defined by my husband's status. If I had divorced my husband in that small town, some people would have looked askance at me and of course everybody would want to know all about it. No privacy. I have a lot more freedom, a lot more choices than my mother ever dreamed of having. If only I could find some way of handling all these freedoms, all these choices, all these responsibilities without them becoming such an intolerable burden! Why can't I get my act together? Why is it that everything I do seems to conflict with something else? Why can't there be some way to integrate them all, to integrate myself?

## The Need for God

What is happening to Sandra is what happens to many people today. They are essentially good people who want to live "good" lives. They want to make choices on the basis of the right values.

But faced with myriads of right choices, they can't seem to find
the key that will put the choices into a manageable perspective.
The result is not only that they cannot decide between a variety
of values; they have also lost a sense of their own value. They
wonder what is truly good. They wonder what it means to "be
good."

Glenn Tinder, a professor of political science in Boston, recently wrote a provocative article: "Can We Be Good Without
God?"[1] Tinder's answer is: No, we can't be good without God.
His reason is that values need what he calls "a transcendental
backing." We must begin, he says, with the belief that we are created by God and that we are therefore "intrinsically mysterious,"
that we are granted "glory" — a "participation in the goodness of
all that has been created." We all have value. "All are sacred,"
says Tinder. "None are good." This sacredness delivers us from
the tyranny of a fickle society constantly changing the rules and
standards so that we can never ultimately feel worthy or accepted
for who we are.

By insisting that goodness — and values — begin with a sense
of transcendence, with God, Tinder helps us get a perspective
on our problem of fragmentation. He is helping people like Sandra transcend their obsession with making the right choices by
showing that we need, first of all, some overall point of view.

Some inner hunch may have led Sandra to hope that her conflict had to do with recovering a religious faith. Her desire to get
her life together may stem from a sense that integration has ultimately to do with some kind of faith in God, with something
more than her immediate concerns.

## Our Many Gods

Religion begins with a sense of transcendence. This sense of the
"Wholly Other," a power beyond this world that nevertheless has
a lot to do with what happens in this world and those who live
in it took many centuries to develop. Sometimes it instilled more
fear than peace in people's hearts. In some cultures the deities
were dreaded as forces arrayed against humans. The gods might
be divided against each other and could cause people to be divided within themselves as they tried to satisfy more than one.

[1]Glenn Tinder, "Can We Be Good without God?" *Atlantic Monthly*, December
1989.

Yet people might be afraid not to worship more than one god for fear of being punished by those they had rejected. They resorted to some form of polytheism, the worship of many gods.

We can be caught in the same dilemma. People like Sandra seem to live under the tyranny of too many gods, gods who will not share her devotion with other gods, gods who all demand all of her. Work, in our day, has often become a god that demands our total allegiance. It is intolerant of devotion given to family or self or social causes or recreation.

But partners, children and friends also make demands. Such demands may well be quite legitimate and are not easily silenced by the all-consuming demands of work. Some relationships can become too demanding or one may conflict with another. In Sandra's mother's day, a middle-class woman's career was assumed to be to support her husband's career. Sandra now felt otherwise. But having been brought up with her mother's "god," she felt guilty and threatened when she rejected that god.

Our values, like our gods, seem to have originated with our culture. We inherit them. So has it always been. It seems clear that the ancient Hebrews began as pagans, like the other clans around them. They developed their own clan gods to which they were devoted and which, they thought, took special care of them. Jacob swore by "the Fear of Isaac," while Jacob's uncle Laban swore by "the God of Nahor" (Genesis 31:53). That is, each swore by the God of his father.

### Yahweh Is God

In the wilderness the Hebrews had come to worship a God they called Yahweh. They saw Yahweh primarily as a God who went before them and helped fight their battles. But then, when most of their battles had been fought, this nomadic people settled in Canaan. As farmers, they needed more than a war god. They needed a god of fertility. Such a god already existed and was being worshiped by the Canaanites, who called him "Baal." Many Hebrews saw no reason not to simply add Baal as a god they could also worship.

Others refused this easy accommodation, but it took a prophet called Elijah to challenge that assumption publicly. It was not easy. Baal was the god of the queen, Jezebel, and so had royal approval. But Elijah saw that Baal worship was not compatible with the worship of Yahweh. Yahweh was a "righteous" God and demanded righteousness from worshipers. Yahweh had given commandments showing how to live as a righteous community. Yahweh would not stand, for example, for the sexual practices required by Baal's fertility cult worship.

Elijah, whose very name meant "Yahweh is God!," called together all the people, including the 450 prophets of Baal, on top of Mt. Carmel. He said to his people: "How long will you go limping with two different opinions? If Yahweh is God, follow Yahweh; but if Baal, then follow Baal" (1 Kings 18:21*). "Limping" implies trying to walk on two different levels at the same time, or hopping from one leg to another. The people refused to answer.

Then Elijah, standing alone, invites the prophets of Baal to call on their god to bring down fire from heaven to devour the sacrifice that has been laid. All day they call but with no results. Elijah mocks their god and urges them to call louder: perhaps Baal is asleep! Then Elijah prays to Yahweh and the fire descends. The people fall on their faces and cry: "Yahweh indeed is God; Yahweh indeed is God" (v. 39*).

As another sign of Yahweh's power, it is Yahweh, not Baal, the so-called god of fertility, who sends rain to end the long drought.[2] Elijah is proving not only that Yahweh is more powerful than Baal but that Yahweh, who helps them in battle, is also the God who helps them grow crops. There are not different gods for different functions. There is but one, all-inclusive God.

After such a triumph we might suppose that Elijah could walk fearlessly about the kingdom. Not so. Elijah now flees for his life and hides in a cave. He knows that while Baal has been discredited, the queen is still very much alive and wields great power. He knows she will have his life if she can catch him.

## Practicing Polytheists

We are not talking ancient history here. A recent popular movie, *Wall Street*, showed its main character, a very successful businessman, speaking to his corporation's shareholders. Greed is good, he said. Greed works. Greed is responsible for so many of our great

---

[2]See 1 Kings 18:41–46. Elijah's confrontation with the prophets of Baal is in the same chapter, vv. 17–40.

human accomplishments. Any who dared to expose the fallacy of that argument would have found themselves in a tiny, despised minority. Or suppose that when Sandra applied her values to her budget, she decided to reject the popular customs that children must follow the latest trend in clothes or attend the events that everybody else goes to. Can we imagine the ridicule to which she and her teenagers would be subjected? Can we imagine the anger and resentment of her own children toward her?

Most of us think of ourselves as monotheists. That is, we think we believe in only one God. But in fact, most of us are practicing polytheists. We worship one god in one situation, another god in another situation. On the one hand, we care about the poor and unemployed and homeless and oppressed and may give money to agencies that try to alleviate their conditions. On the other, we may earn our living by working in a system that contributes to that poverty and unemployment and homelessness and oppression. Rarely do we see the contradiction between the two. We are practicing polytheists.

We need not merely to choose between conflicting gods but to choose a God who, as Tinder says, is a transcendent God. Monotheism is not merely choosing one god out of many. It is choosing one God who transcends all gods. That God has a definitive character. That character may well accept or include some of the attributes of the lesser gods, as well as rejecting those gods whose characteristics conflict with it. That is why Elijah could see Yahweh being the God who, like Baal, could cause crops to grow. But Baal, unlike Yahweh, cared little about righteousness. It is not a coincidence that it is Elijah, the prophet of Yahweh, who challenges King Ahab when he has expropriated a poor man's vineyard to enlarge his own garden and has done it by having the man put to death. It is Elijah, not a prophet of Baal, who has the courage to confront the king. "Have you found me, O my enemy?" asks Ahab. "I have found you," replies Elijah. "Because you have sold yourself to do what is wrong in the eyes of the Lord, I will bring disaster upon you..." (1 Kings 21:20–21). Jezebel, Ahab's wife, the champion of Baal, had told Ahab that being king meant he could do as he pleased. Elijah told Ahab that all powers, and all gods, were subject to God, without exception.

It is faith in this transcendent God that gives us courage to challenge some of the values that our culture holds. When a cultural value is made absolute, it becomes an idol. What we have created we now worship. The value may not, in itself, be evil. It may be good and therefore all the more attractive. But when it is set above criticism, then it has taken to itself powers that do not belong to it. And when several values claim such powers and we bow down before them all, our lives are caught in the inevitable conflict. We also lose that quality of transcendence which, as Tinder says, must precede values.

## A God of Steadfast Love

When Christians speak of values and of standards, they usually point to the Ten Commandments. But what is often forgotten is the brief but all-important introduction to the Ten Commandments: "Then God spoke all these words: I am the Lord your God, who brought you out of the land of Egypt, out of the house of slavery" (Exodus 20:1–2).

This introduction sets the commandments in the context of a long-standing, redemptive relationship between God and God's people. Values, standards, commandments, cannot be separated from their source. Ultimately, they derive their validity from the faith we put in their source. The values about to be enunciated were no mere human edicts; they came directly from God. But they were not demands imposed from the outside upon one and all. They marked a relationship, a covenant, to which both God and the people were committed.

There can be little doubt that these values had been hammered out over many years. Similar precepts were found in other ancient Near Eastern codes. But their validity still depends on God as their ultimate source. That is why the first commandment is and must be: "You shall have no other gods before [or besides] me" (Exodus 20:3). This is not merely the demand of a jealous god who cannot tolerate competition. It is the strong statement that if a universe is to exist, it must have a coherent center. If humanity is to have a purpose, it must be guided by consistent principles. And if a person is to be one, integral person, she or he must have one God to follow.

Monotheism, the worship of one God, is not knuckling under to an Omnipotent Force. It is the free choice of the kind of God we can with integrity believe in: a God we can love and trust with all our hearts. That was the kind of God the Hebrews had come to know in Yahweh. In its earliest form the covenant made with the Hebrews seemed to say only that God would never leave them, that God would be the God who not only delivered them out of slavery and called them to a land of plenty and freedom, but also a God who was ever-present. Outside their wilderness camp, Moses pitched a special tent and called it a "tent of meeting," a place to meet God. Anyone who sought God could go there. There God talked with Moses, face to face, as a person talks with a friend (Exodus 33:7–11).

It was this God who, before re-inscribing the Ten Commandments on stone tablets, offered this self-description to Moses:

> The Lord, the Lord,
> a God merciful and gracious,
> slow to anger,
> and abounding in steadfast love and faithfulness.
> (Exodus 34:6b; see also Psalm 103:7–8).

It was this kind of God that Sandra was looking for when she came to the study group at the church. She had had enough of gods whose main concern seemed to be to find people guilty. She had had more than enough of competing gods whose demands tore her apart. She was not seeking a faith without demands, one that offered an easy way out. She would welcome direction, but it must be given by one who began by genuinely caring for her.

Sandra's soul cried out for a loving God whom she could truly love. Perhaps she would be surprised to know how common such longing is, and how ancient. A psalm of the Hebrews expresses it well:

> As a deer longs for flowing streams,
>     so my soul longs for you, O God.
> My soul thirsts for God,
>     for the living God.
> When shall I come and behold the face of God?...
>
> By day the Lord commands God's steadfast love;
>     and at night God's song is with me,
> a prayer to the God of my life.
>
> (Psalm 42:1–2, 8*)

"A God of steadfast love" — that is what we all need. Our God must not only be transcendent, above all gods. Our God, the One who will unite everything that is good and help us unite ourselves as persons, must be the God of transcendent love.

## Jesus Makes Decisions

This is the God whom Jesus revealed so clearly. Often Jesus is presented to us as a person who always made the right choices, who always had life sorted out properly.

Yet such a person might only make us feel our fragmentation more keenly. But in the Gospels we also see a person harassed with many complex decisions, needing not just to sort the good from the bad but to put good values in proper order.

Early in his public life we see him under great tension and pressure. In the desert he had to resist the temptation to do the right things for the wrong reasons, like feeding the hungry in order to prove he was good or powerful. Perhaps he had had to stand testings even earlier. Tradition says that Joseph died when Jesus was young. Perhaps he had wanted to leave home to begin his vocation as a teacher of the Kingdom of God. But if the family depended on him as the eldest child for support, he might have had to delay his dream, his very life's calling. Such decisions are not lightly made.

He must often have wondered whether he should make better friends among influential people of his day, people who were devoted to God's way but believed it was followed by keeping the ancient laws. Jesus also believed in those laws. He believed that not the tiniest part of one of them would be erased, ever. But he believed we must go beyond the laws in the direction they pointed, to a more inclusive love. To be true to that conviction he might have to offend these sincere, good people and demonstrate his beliefs by making friends with people shunned as "lawbreakers." He would be misunderstood. He would hurt good people, perhaps alienate his most natural allies. What was right? What was the way of love? He had no manual to consult. He had to make his decision on the basis of his relationship to a God of love. No wonder he did not merely study the ancient moral laws. He also spent long hours alone with God in prayer, sweating it out.

And he never could be sure that he was right. In his last great decision, made in a garden called Gethsemane, he sweated blood. Was it right to risk almost certain death in order to prove that God loves people to the very end, no matter how sinful they are? Or should he ease up a bit and give himself a little longer to explain his beliefs? We all know his decision. But even after he had made it, he apparently had doubts. On the cross, paying the price of his decision, he cried that most poignant of all cries: "My God, my God, why hast thou forsaken me?" Did he think he had made a mistake?

### The Two Commandments

Those of us who want more foolproof certainty than that may well be disturbed by this scenario. Yet, in our hearts, we know that Jesus' way has more integrity. A wonderful quality of the Hebrew Scriptures is that they are not afraid to depict God as wondering what is the right thing to do. When people seem to be hopelessly corrupt, God destroys them with a flood. Then God regrets the destruction that followed that decision. Apparently God sees, in retrospect, that the choice was wrong. Why? Because, if God truly loves the human beings God has made, then God must love them to the end. So God makes a covenant with imperfect people and puts a rainbow in the sky to remind God of that covenant.

Jesus insisted, however, that all this talk about love and making decisions does not rule out the Ten Commandments. When someone asked him which commandments were most important, he recited a summary that had been made generations before. "You shall love the Lord your God with all your heart, and with all your soul, and with all your mind." To this he added a summary of the laws concerning responsibility to others: "You shall love your neighbor as yourself." "On these two commandments," said Jesus, "hang all the law and the prophets" (Matthew 22:37–40).

In this summary, Jesus condenses all good values into only two: Love God, and love your neighbor. If we love God with our whole being, we will resist the temptation to give allegiance to other gods whose nature is less than love. And if we love our neighbors as ourselves we will understand that we will not kill them, steal from them, profane their relationships, covet what they have or besmirch their reputations. *The commandments then, are not so much a check on our evil impulses as an expression of our loving inclinations.*

Those who are loved by God must also love themselves. That is, we must celebrate the sacredness of our beings. This value is crucial in an age when life seems so hectic, and when so many demands, most of them legitimate, are made on us. We begin to see a new and positive meaning for the commandment to "remember the Sabbath day and keep it holy." The command does not prohibit enjoyment one day a week but reminds us that after six days of creative work, God needed to rest also. The Sabbath is a symbol. We all need time to remember that our being is made in the image of the Sacred One. We need holy time to stay holy.

These reflections may not seem to respond to the immediate needs of people in particular circumstances. Yet all guidelines for decisions need a transcendent perspective. The times have changed and will continue to change. We need living values, values that come from the living source, that have been handed down to us as living, dynamic truths, and values that we, in turn, must keep alive as we apply them to our situations. Because these values are dynamic, they are not to be applied in a rigid, legalistic way, but with the flexibility that love affirms. People like Sandra, beset with many demands, may have to make compromises in how they spend their time and energy. But compromise is not necessarily bad. It may be a way of putting demands in their proper place.

## Principalities and Powers

"Putting things in their proper place" is a very spiritual activity. It is a form of devotion to the God of love. Walter Wink has written extensively about pressure from the "powers" all about us. By "powers" he means all those forces that make ultimate demands on us. They may be institutions, like the state, or cultural values, like materialism and consumerism. Powers may be good and necessary in themselves; it is when they put themselves above God's purpose for the good of the whole that they become idolatrous and demonic.

Wink says that the church's task is to unmask this idolatry and to recall the powers to their created purposes in the world, that is, to put them in their place under God. He quotes from the Letter to the Ephesians: "so that the Sovereignties and Powers should learn, only now, through the Church, how comprehensive God's wisdom really is" (Ephesians 3:10, JB).[3]

A similar message is given in the Letter to the Colossians. The writer is concerned that people learn to know God better and demonstrate that knowledge by living lives of active goodness. That sounds like what most of us want, too. The writer says we are helped in this aspiration by looking to the person of Jesus. Jesus reminds us of what God is like. Then he goes on to say that Jesus has been given primacy over all created things, whether they be visible or invisible, thrones or powers. Jesus is, as it were, the integrating force that holds everything together. In him all things in heaven and on earth are "reconciled," or "held together" (see Colossians 1:10–20). In Jesus, God is holding our lives together, saving us from fragmentation by helping us to assign a place, a proper priority, to the many demands made upon us. We are enabled to control our lives from within, rather than being controlled by a thousand competing forces from without. We begin to experience a taste of what the Letter to the Ephesians called God's "comprehensive wisdom."

The Swiss psychologist Carl Jung emphasized our need for this kind of integration. He speaks of a kind of "wholeness," "in which all the different elements of the psyche, both conscious and unconscious, are welded together."[4] This quest for integration is, he says, a spiritual journey and the integrating factor is named the Self. But the Self, as Jung perceives it, "is a God-image, or at least cannot be distinguished from one."[5] It is essential, says Jung, that we hold at arm's length the various deities that want us to serve and worship them. " 'Principalities and powers' are always with us," Jung continues. "We have no need to create them even if we could. It is merely incumbent on us to *choose* the master we wish to serve, so that his service shall be our safeguard against being mastered by the 'other' whom we have not chosen. We do not *create* 'God,' we *choose* him."[6]

---

[3]Walter Wink, *Naming the Powers: The Language of Power in the New Testament* (Philadelphia: Fortress Press, 1984).

[4]*The Essential Jung*, selected and introduced by Anthony Storr (Princeton: Princeton University Press, 1983), p. 229.

[5]Jung, *Collected Works* 9, ii, par. 2, quoted in Storr, ibid.

[6]From "Psychology and Religion," quoted in Storr, ibid., p. 246.

## Modern Idols

Not to choose our God is to allow other gods to hold sway in our lives, thus leading to fragmentation and idolatry. The ancient Book of Wisdom, an apocryphal writing, understood this. "The idea of making idols," it said, "was the beginning of fornication.... And this became a hidden trap for humankind, because people, in bondage to misfortune or to royal authority, bestowed on objects of stone or wood the name that ought not to be shared" (Wisdom of Solomon 14:12a, 21). The result was that although people lived in great strife, they called it peace (14:22).

When the overarching sovereignty of God is not acknowledged, many idols rush in to fill the vacuum. The tragedy is that none of them is large enough to fill the void, but they try to inflate themselves to do so. In our day, science can be such an idol. Its "power" has given us many wonderful new technologies: we have been able to send people to walk on the moon and satellites to photograph Mars. Scientific knowledge also allowed people to produce nuclear bombs — enough of them to destroy the whole earth. Nations trusted that the fear that power produced to keep "peace" for the last two generations. While we knelt at the shrine of that power, almost as many millions died from starvation as might have been destroyed by the bomb. But the bomb produced by the high priests of science was the idol that claimed a trillion dollars a year and gave a new meaning to "sacrificial offering." Yet, now that the bomb's impotence to bring us real peace is exposed, many still trust science and technology as saviors.

Modern medicine, which has worked such miracles for us, can also be an idol. With the increasing incidence of organ transplants, many look to medical science to avoid their mortality. They look for technical cures instead of spiritual healing. They substitute physical repairs and replacements for participation in "eternal life."

Nationalism is one of the most common forms of idolatry. In our changing times the whole face of the world is being radically altered. Who will be the Great Powers in the next decade or two, now that shifting political and economic forces seem to be demoting the USSR and the U.S. to the status of more "ordinary" large nations? But why does *any* nation need to be a "Great Power"? Nationalism is the idolatry that fills the gap when nations fail to think globally. The world reverberates with cries for help. Eastern European countries and the Soviet Union desperately need economic aid, as do China and other Asian countries like the Philippines. Some Latin American and African countries like Ethiopia and the Sudan need help just to survive. After World War II the Marshall Plan provided $12.8 billion from 1948 to 1952 to rebuild Western Europe. There is no such plan for our day.

Meanwhile, in the two-thirds world, 5 of every 1,000 children will die before the age of 5, 4 out of every 10 will never reach grade eight, and 150 million are malnourished. Most of this death and suffering could be abolished by transferring even a small percentage of the money the world spends on arms. A Summit for Children sponsored by the United Nations through UNICEF in October 1990 asked world leaders to commit themselves to cutting the death rate for children under five in half by the year 2000. UNICEF estimates this would cost $2 billion to $3 billion a year, over the next decade. This is but a small percentage of the amount presently being spent on arms, but to make the transfer of even this amount would symbolize a redemptive shift in nations' values to world needs instead of national power.

In addition, the UNICEF conference urged participants to ratify the U.N. Convention on the Rights of the Child. That convention sets minimum standards for the survival, health and education of children, as well as against exploitation and abuse. The idea received general approval but little real commitment. Such proposals seem small in relation to the world's needs and the world's resources, but even such conferences are a hymn to the God who loves all creation. To act on the proposals and begin to care for all our children would mark a turning away from the idols that have so profaned our world and our worship for so long.

## Signs of Transcendence

Similarly, while remaining realistic about the power of even discredited idols, we should welcome any indication that idols and the values they represent are being assigned to their proper places. In the battle for the health of the environment, for example, we can do some preliminary rejoicing that industries are at last beginning to accept some responsibility, acknowledging that profit cannot be valued above the future of the planet. Some industries are hiring persons with environmental training. Some oil companies say they will acquire only double-hull tankers to reduce the likelihood of oil spills. Three major U.S. tuna canners announced they would buy only tuna caught by methods that don't also kill dolphins. Large newspapers have committed themselves to use only recycled paper as soon as they can be assured of an adequate supply. We may regard these initiatives as only a drop in the bucket, but they are signs that public opinion can have an effect and that policies will change as priorities change — as more "transcendent" goals replace more individualistic and temporary ones.

We can be among those who watch for such signs of transcendence, signs that people can rise above single issues to consider several concerns, signs of more integration, less fragmentation. Consider the trend toward interracial coalitions in U.S. politics. Black governors have been elected, black mayors have come to power, in areas where blacks make up only a quarter or less of the population. In other words, it is possible for voters to move from the issue of race to concerns that are inclusive of all races. That is a move toward the "transcendent" criterion of loving one's neighbor, all neighbors, as oneself. It is a move toward the transcendence of Martin Luther King's God, who made and loves all races, over the idols of racism.

As Jung (and Elijah) emphasized, we must choose our God. That God transcends all other gods and puts them in their place. An ultimate allegiance allows us to set priorities. Thus a God who cares for the whole world puts nationalism in its place and makes true patriotism possible. In its proper place, patriotism encourages us to love what may be unique to our country without claiming supremacy for it. A God who cares for human beings as reflections of God puts science, medicine and defense of a nation at the service of human beings. A God who cares for all creation puts the making of profit below the preservation of the environment. A God who made all races celebrates the uniqueness of each but also cherishes the contribution each makes to the whole human race.

## Wholeness

When we are called to choose our God, therefore, we reject some gods that are simply "out of character" for our God. Gods characterized by violence, hate, greed, self-seeking power, racism and sexism cannot be worshiped alongside the God of peace and love for all. As Jesus said: "No one can serve two masters" (Matthew 6:24). A part of our journey to integrity, then, will consist in committing ourselves more completely to the God we have come to know in Jesus Christ and in rejecting those elements in us and in our society that conflict with that God. When society approves values we feel called to reject, the choice will be doubly hard. As we reject unworthy values, we ourselves may feel rejected.

At the same time that integration leads us to exclude certain values, it calls us to be more inclusive. We see this most clearly when we come to decide which parts of ourselves we can include or accept. We have noted how Jesus, while honoring every one of the laws, nevertheless seemed comfortable as he kept company with "lawbreakers." He also chose very imperfect people as disciples. Do we gather from this that we are called to accept those parts of ourselves, the parts Jung calls "the shadow side," as an integral part of us along with the side we approve of?

When we think of integration as "wholeness" or "completeness," it is hard to think of rejecting any part of ourselves, just as it is hard to reject any members of our community. Perhaps, in the name of accepting only that part of ourselves that is "good" we have been guilty of a kind of idolatry of goodness. That is, we have put the goal of moral perfection ahead of the goal of accepting our whole selves.

The same passage that speaks of Jesus putting things in their proper places and holding all things together (Colossians 1:15–19) also says that in Christ God "reconciled" all things to God — everything on earth and in heaven. This seems to bear out Peter's emphasis in a sermon in Jerusalem (Acts 3:11–26). There he urges the people to repent so that "times of refreshing" may come from God and God will fulfill the time of "universal restoration that God announced long ago through then holy prophets" (v. 21*).

We seem, then, to have two contradictory visions existing side by side in the Scriptures. On the one hand, as in the scene of judgment Jesus pictures (Matthew 25:31–46), people are separated like sheep from goats into good and evil, on the basis of compassion. On the other hand, the Bible gives us visions of a universe in which all is reconciled. But perhaps these two concepts represent what we know to be reality. We do have to distinguish between right and wrong and make choices based on that distinction. But we also must recognize that the two do exist together and that "wholeness" is violated when they are too rigidly separated. Jung says that when a person tries to put together apparently irreconcilable opposites and bridge over apparently hopeless splits, there is a certain therapeutic effect — that even to attempt it is a healing exercise. This agonizing wholeness is much more difficult than the simple compartmentalization of right and wrong, but it is the only way to integration as individuals or as communities. Just as we are called to love the sinner as a member of society, we are called to love the sinner who is ourself.[7]

## Overcoming Separation

As we do this, we are expressing the kind of inclusiveness that goes with the character of an all-loving God. It helps us see that God does not judge us by adding up the sum total of our good deeds and bad deeds. Rather our goal is to seek after the character of God, to walk in God's ways, to set a "godly" direction for ourselves. Along the way we may make many wrong decisions, follow dead-end roads and at times perhaps even give up. But in the end a certain consistent *pattern* or *direction* can be discerned. The *goal* has been kept in mind. We have walked "with integrity of heart" (Psalm 101:2).

But one more difficulty confronts us as we strive for integration. We know that we must make decisions. But we also know that many decisions are made for us. Sandra was placed in a situation that was, to a large extent, not of her own making. And most of the world lives with much less freedom of choice than Sandra has.

Dorothee Sölle quotes from a letter written by an Indonesian father.[8] The father says that his family is so poor that his wife has to work as a virtual slave for pennies a day while her children are left at home unattended. One daughter has become a prostitute in order to help the family. "A victim of poverty, my God. I am ashamed," he says. Yet even he and his family have maintained an important degree of integrity. "But the rich society," he says, "can only buy our bodies, not our souls."

---

[7]See Storr, *The Essential Jung*, pp. 256 and 281.
[8]Letter in *Public Forum*, December 14, 1979, quoted by Sölle in "Sin Is When Life Freezes Over," *Christian Century*, May 12, 1982.

In this remarkable statement of faith, the Indonesian father echoes the hope expressed by Paul in his letter to the Romans. Paul has spoken about his own agony in trying to do what he knows is right (Romans 7:14–25). He goes on to speak of the agony of the whole of creation as it struggles for redemption and new birth. Paul says the Spirit of God is with us in this struggle and that God's Spirit intercedes for us when we do not even know what to pray for. But Paul is firm in his faith that, in the end, nothing can destroy our oneness with God, which is the ultimate integrity:

> What then are we to say about these things? If God is for us, who is against us? ... in all these things we are more than conquerors through [Christ] who loved us. For I am convinced that neither death, nor life, nor angels, nor rulers, nor things present, nor things to come, nor powers, nor height, nor depth, nor anything else in all creation, will be able to separate us from the love of God in Christ Jesus our Lord" (Romans 8:31, 37–39).

In this uplifting hymn, Paul points us to the Christ who, in spite of all the forces arrayed against him, refused to be a victim. Though nailed to a cross, he had found wholeness in the embrace of a God of love.

# 6

*threat* / *fulfillment*

# *How do we view the future?*

DAVID SUZUKI is a scientist and a passionate environmentalist. In October 1989, he was speaking at a children's environmental festival in Toronto. It was a beautiful day and the sponsors of the festival had set up a series of games on the grounds.

The object of the festival was to help children realize serious ecological issues "in positive and nonthreatening ways." Suzuki wanted to join in the celebrative mood, but as he stood to speak to the three hundred or so parents and children he could not conceal his profound concern. "Ever since human beings evolved on this planet about 800,000 years ago," he said, "every generation of parents, of grown-ups, has hoped that their children might have a little better opportunity than they did, a little better life — at least their children would have a greater hope for something in the future. Today, for the first time in human history, we as parents know with absolute certainty that our children will not have more opportunities than we did when we were children."[1]

People criticized Suzuki for "crying wolf," but Suzuki replied: "We've heard about the boy who cried wolf, but the whole point about the parable, it seems to me, is that in the end, the wolf did come. I don't think we can afford to take the chance that maybe we are crying wolf at the wrong time." As he spoke, Suzuki's concern rose to rage as he contemplated the probability that an "absolute catastrophe" will occur in the next thirty years. "He spoke about PCBs,... the loss of topsoil, the decline of food crops,

---

[1]David Lees, "A Man Who Cries Wolf," *Harrowsmith* magazine, March–April 1990.

the thinning of the ozone layer, the greenhouse effect, the rise in ocean levels and the demise of the world's rain forests."[2]

> And then he told the children the parable of the frog that cannot detect gradual temperature changes in water. "If you take a frog and put it into a pot of cold water and then you put that water on a hotplate and gradually heat it up, the frog will just sit there because it can't tell that anything is different. If you tell that frog, 'Mr. Frog, you'd better get out of there,' the frog will say, 'I'm fine, what are you talking about? Nothing's wrong.' And that frog will sit there until it boils to death because it can't tell the difference. And we are like the frog in many ways. We are sitting here, and we simply can't tell what the great hazards to our survival are."

### Interpreting the Facts

When Jesus spoke of what he saw happening in the future, even the destruction of the beloved city of Jerusalem, people begged him: "Tell us, when will this happen? And what will be the signal for your coming and the end of the age?" Jesus described some signs, as Suzuki did. But then he said:

> "For as the days of Noah were, so will be the coming of the Son of Man. For as in those days before the flood they were eating and drinking, marrying and giving in marriage, until the day Noah entered the ark, and they knew nothing until the flood came and swept them all away, so too will be the coming of the Son of Man.... Keep awake, therefore, for you do not know on what day your Lord is coming" (Matthew 24:37–39, 42).

When we add to the gloomy prospects for the environment our world's massive political, economic and social ills, we look to the future with fear and trembling. And that fear could be very healthy, if it led us to repent of humanity's great wrongs and to transform our way of life. But if our fear only paralyzed us, or drove us to thinking only of our own survival, it would only hasten and aggravate the catastrophe.

---

[2]Ibid., p. 36.

Other ways of viewing the future can be equally destructive. Not only can we be unaware of what is going on, as was the frog in Suzuki's parable, we can also misinterpret what is happening. A friend who piloted an Allied bomber in World War II told me that when his crew was returning to England after completing a run over Germany, they were attacked by a German fighter plane. Over the intercom the pilots heard the excited voice of the gunner in the tail of the plane. He had been shooting at the attacking plane and shouted ecstatically: "I got him! I got him!" What he did not know was that the enemy had also hit his plane! They were on fire and on their way down.

Some people look at events in our world today and see a victory for "our side." Either they are unaware of the real facts or they misinterpret them. They view political and economic collapse in the Soviet Union and in Eastern Europe as the defeat of communism by capitalism. But they overlook fatal weaknesses that could well lead to the collapse of "our" system. A cartoon shows three well-to-do men speaking to a wretched beggar huddling in the gutter. One says: " 'Tis the season to be jolly, my good man! We *won* — did you know that? Capitalism is triumphant. Communism lies in ruins. Our system prevails! We won! Smile!" The poor beggar mumbles: "Well, I never."[3]

When the Pharisees and Sadducees asked Jesus for a sign from heaven, he said: "When it is evening, you say, 'It will be fair weather, for the sky is red.' And in the morning, 'It will be stormy today, for the sky is red and threatening.' You know how to interpret the appearance of the sky, but you cannot interpret the signs of the times' " (Matthew 16:3). According to the sequence in Matthew's Gospel, Jesus had just healed the daughter of a Gentile woman, made the dumb speak, the maimed whole, the lame walk and the blind see, after which he had fed a hungry multitude with seven loaves and a few small fish. The Pharisees and Sadducees asked for a sign from heaven, but they had failed to see, to understand, the signs all around them.

Small wonder that we fail to see the magnitude of some of the changes taking place in our day, let alone understand them. The political changes alone are so overwhelming and so recent it is impossible to get much perspective on them. Some are saying

---

[3]*Manchester Guardian Weekly*, February 4, 1990.

the year 1989 will go down in history as *annus mirabilis*, a year of wonders. We sense that the familiar shape of the world is now unrecognizable, and we can only guess what it will look like in the future. It is as if we are staring into a void.[4]

At the same time, other developments have been taking place that threaten our environment, cut our social programs and increase poverty, and most people have failed to see them. What can we do to begin to understand what is happening, so that we may find some clues about how we may respond?

### Beyond Stereotypes

The first step is to recognize that we have tended to think in stereotypes. When, for example, we described the world as simply a battle between capitalism and communism, we failed to see how simplistic such an analysis is. As J. K. Galbraith points out, the communism that failed was not the communism that Marx envisaged.[5] Marx was responding to a capitalism that he thought would inevitably fail, because of the great gap in power and income between employers and workers. He saw the recurring depressions into which millions were thrown, angry and impoverished. He hoped to bring about a state with equality, security, power and plenty for all. As practiced in the USSR, however, communism created a huge bureaucracy that was incapable of adapting to change and that concentrated power and privilege in itself. It collapsed. The reforms that Gorbachev and others are struggling so hard to set in motion and control are attempts not simply to import models from other societies, but to return to some more inclusive ideals of communism's early theorists and leaders.[6]

Capitalism survived partly because it was able to adapt. Governments took some responsibility in controlling, to a degree, the fluctuations in business cycles that brought suffering to so many. Capitalism, under pressure, was modified. While some forms of capitalism retained glaring injustices, other forms became more responsive to social needs.

---

[4]See A. J. Conyers, "Communism's Collapse," *Christian Century*, May 2, 1990.

[5]J. K. Galbraith, "Why the Right Is Wrong," *Manchester Guardian Weekly*, February 4, 1990.

[6]See Orlando Figis in *Manchester Guardian Weekly*, May 13, 1990.

Nevertheless, the Cold War relied on the stereotypes of capitalism and communism to give us some sense of security. The world was divided "neatly" and balanced "evenly" between the communists and us. If we were not always sure who "we" were, we thought we knew who the enemy was, and that seemed enough. Now our nations, which had in part defined themselves as staunchly against communism, are not sure how to look at themselves or to be friends with erstwhile enemies. Our stereotypes have failed us!

The second step is to look for what lies beneath and beyond the stereotypes. What new patterns are coming into being? We can recognize that as the Cold War winds down, a new internationalism may be emerging. In the future many nations may contribute not only power, but ideas and values to the world scene. Radical changes took place in Eastern Europe without the direct initiative of either East or West. The changes seemed largely to be inspired internally, although undoubtedly influenced by events in the Soviet Union. Many were excited and inspired by these changes and now ask: "What values do we have to offer to this new internationalism?"

The question embarrasses us. In asking it, we realize that we must take a third step. We need to see what values are represented by the patterns we have observed, both those that produced the stereotypes and the new emerging patterns. In this case, we need to become aware of how widespread is the overconsumption, the waste, the greed, the self-centeredness, the callousness to the needy in our countries and elsewhere. This awareness leads to yet another one: while we seemed able to protect ourselves with a huge arsenal of arms, we seem impotent to create a nation of noble ideals and imaginative responses to our critical world situation. We may recall Stanley Hoffman's statement: "We cannot replace a fading vision — that of containment — with mere short-term management and avoidance of trouble, because the present offers opportunities for a decisive change in direction, and because there are simply too many dangers ahead to allow us to stumble from issue to issue in a 'pragmatic' way."[7]

Finally, we need to see if those values are integrated by a vi-

---

[7] See above, p. 4.

sion, a vision complete and compelling enough to inspire us. And for us, that vision needs to transcend the situations that have produced our questions; it must be related to God's creative purpose for the world.

As we look at our societies amid international change today, many of us feel that our deeply ingrained stereotypes and our obsession with material possessions have left us without any such real vision to inspire and direct us. The Pentagon seems prepared to fight to preserve the status quo, to insist that the enemy is still there and that, if it isn't, there must be another one somewhere. George Bush expresses uneasiness with "the vision thing." "Yet," as Hugo Young puts it,

> if... the Cold War is to produce a real peace dividend and a reordering of American priorities, some presidential vision of the new world is a necessary preliminary. This, in turn, would require us to be challenged by competing visions in a fully articulated national debate. Of that... there is no sign. It is a weakness.... Unless [we] rediscover the art of political courage [to change the status quo] the greatest domestic crisis will remain unresolved.[8]

### New Wine, New Wineskins

Can we hear in this challenge an echo of another of Jesus' sayings?

> "No one sews a piece of unshrunk cloth on an old cloak; otherwise, the patch pulls away from it, the new from the old, and a worse tear is made. And no one puts new wine into old wineskins; otherwise, the wine will burst the skins, and the wine is lost, and so are the skins; but one puts new wine into fresh wineskins" (Mark 2:21–22).

But where are new wine and new wineskins to be found for our changing world? When we stop to think, we realize that our values do fluctuate and that new values, both for societies and for persons, do in fact replace old ones. We could conclude that

---

[8]Hugo Young, "A New World Vision Mired in the Status Quo," *Manchester Guardian Weekly*, May 27, 1990.

history merely repeats itself, that old wine is simply recycled and becomes new wine. Nations rise and fall. Values come and go.

But why do values come and go? Why do new values rise? Is there a moral ebb and flow that we should accept as inevitable? Certainly those brave persons who served years in the prisons of Czechoslovakia — and of South Africa and Argentina and many other countries — for the sake of their faith would protest that kind of passive resignation. The political changes we are seeing in our day come in response to an unseen, unsuspected fire in the hearts of many men and women, a vision they could no longer suppress. As we look for what we can contribute to our changing times, where can we find a vision that can inspire us with "living values"? Can we envision a society that is not neatly divided into stereotypes, one that understands that most systems have the potential for both good and evil and need constantly to be reviewed and renewed, a society that subordinates material goods to more spiritual qualities, a society that is able to judge its present condition while beckoning us to a future community where there is justice for all and where war will be banished?

For Christians, such a vision takes shape in what we call "the Reign of God," often translated "Kingdom of God." Jesus Christ was, above all, the Proclaimer of the Reign of God. God's Reign was the central theme of his teaching; it shaped how he saw his vocation and all he did to fulfill it. Jesus' message about the Reign of God, then, not only guides how Christians view the future but how we view ourselves as persons. In Jesus' message, self-fulfillment walks hand in hand with the "fulfillment" of the world.

## The Reign of God

Jesus opens his ministry with the bold challenge: "The time is fulfilled, and the kingdom of God has come near; repent, and believe in the good news" (Mark 1:15). The word used for "time" is *kairos*, which means not a date on the calendar but a moment and situation of critical opportunity and fulfillment. Jesus' "time" referred to the day the prophets of old had spoken of, looked forward to and worked for. It was the day when God's will would be done on earth as it is done in heaven. To be sure, the day was only just dawning, but already signs of its activity could be seen.

Jesus challenged people to look for those signs and to respond to the claims the signs made on them.

The Reign of God was characterized in who Jesus was and what he did — how he welcomed the outcasts, ate with sinners, healed the sick, forgave the penitent and sacrificed his life for the sake of the world he loved. He described both his vision and his vocation in a manifesto in his home synagogue at Nazareth. He read these words from the prophet Isaiah:

> "The spirit of the Lord is upon me,
>    because God has anointed me
>       to bring good news to the poor.
> God has sent me to proclaim
>    release to the captives
> and recovery of sight to the blind,
>    to let the oppressed go free,
> to proclaim the year of the Lord's favor."
>                                (Luke 4:18–19*)

Then he said: "Today, this scripture has been fulfilled in your hearing" (v. 21). In other words, "I am here to tell you that the Reign of God, for which we have yearned so long, has begun."

The Reign of God is not a society we create. It is God's gift. It is not a utopia or a new social order. Nor is it merely a warm feeling of goodness in human hearts. It is an act of God. It is God at work, breaking the power of evil and manifesting the power of love. But we can all have a part in God's gift, God's Reign. This participation is exciting but dangerous. Yet as we realize the costs and endure the setbacks, we share in what Jesus himself willingly experienced. It was in the acts of Jesus, actions in which he felt deeply involved in the Reign of God, that people came to see him as the true Messiah, the true fulfillment of the hopes and dreams of the centuries. As we share Jesus' experience, we also share his vision.

## Longing for Heaven

A vision of a peaceful, just and caring society, a society where people treat one another with the human dignity that all deserve, and where no one lacks the essentials of life, has appealed to many people, both Christians and others. It is a vision that in the modern world many have tried to embody. In fact, the two systems we discussed earlier, communism and capitalism in a democratic setting, have both been seen as paths to such fulfillment.

The founders of communism dreamed of creating a society in which the injustices and inequities of industrial societies would be eradicated. The state they envisioned was, in fact, a secular version of the Kingdom of God. That is what gave it such power and appeal. In spite of its anti-religious stance, communism had a transcendent dimension and inspired people to commitment, hope and a willingness to sacrifice. In a recent article, A. J. Conyers of Baptist College at Charleston, South Carolina, warns against thinking that Eastern Europeans have rejected communism because they were attracted to Western values. Both East and West, he says, are going through a larger crisis "that stems from a world plunging itself into a secularized darkness, a world that has lost its anchor in transcendent values — a world, in short, that has forgotten how it once longed for heaven."[9]

You can hear this "longing for heaven," says Conyers, in the words of the "Internationale," a sort of "apocalyptic hymn":

> Arise, ye prisoners of starvation,
> Arise, ye wretched of the earth,
> For justice thunders condemnation,
> A better world's in birth.
>
> 'Tis the final conflict
> Let each stand in his place,
> The Internationale
> Shall be the human race.

We can hear echoes here of Isaiah's stirring words that Jesus read in Nazareth, although it is clear that the communist hymn challenges human beings to do by themselves what Isaiah and Jesus believe only God can ultimately do. The vision that motivated democratic systems has come to take the words *by themselves* in a different sense. Seeking to ensure dignity, respect and rights to the individual, democracies have been weakened when

---

[9] A. J. Conyers, "Communism's Collapse: The Receding Shadow of Transcendence," *Christian Century*, May 2, 1990.

individuals used those rights for selfish purposes and ignored the common good. But in Jesus' teaching of the Reign of God, each person finds fulfillment in becoming part of God's life and activity. Each finds this vision to be his or her new wine, wine to sustain and "make glad the heart" of the gathered community.

Fortunately, God does not give up on the world or the people who live in it. By grace, God always seems to find some who are ready and eager to recognize new wine and to prepare new wineskins. Erazim Kohak, who teaches philosophy at Boston University, recently returned to Prague after an absence of forty-two years. He is excited about what is happening in Czechoslovakia and hopes that it can give us all some direction as we seek for new ways to envision God's Reign. He knows how appealing a consumer society can be, that full shop windows can seem more attractive than ecological concerns or social justice. But he notes that while North American and European society is becoming increasingly secular, Central Europeans are flocking to church, "rediscovering the world as a morally ordered place." He dares to hope that the Czech vision of "life in truth," "the fundamental conviction that the good is always worth doing," regardless of its utilitarian value, will triumph. "As a Czech philosopher," he says, "I see the task of articulating and preserving that vision as my calling."[10]

## The Depth Dimension

The Czech revolution gives us hope because it is so rooted in a transcendent base. Vaclav Havel, a playwright who had spent many months in jail for his opposition to the communist regime, was elected president at the Hradcany Castle in Prague on December 29, 1989. Havel seems to be aware that all revolutions, all political systems and human institutions, despite their original idealism, can become idols. After a short speech, Havel and some members of parliament crossed the castle compound to St. Vitus Cathedral. There, Cardinal Frantisek Tomasek, archbishop of Prague, celebrated a Te Deum mass. This act seemed to be Havel's way of recognizing human weaknesses along with human aspirations.

---

[10]Erazim Kohak, "What's Central to Central Europe," from *Dissent*, Spring 1990; reprinted in *Harper's*, June 1990.

While Havel's presidency was celebrated in a Roman Catholic cathedral, his roots, and the roots of the revolution he leads, also go back to prophets like Jan Hus, who spoke for the rights of the people against the power of the Latin church. Hus's religion was centered more in moral reform than in ecclesiastical change. After he was burned at the stake in 1410 by the emperor, his spirit continued to energize the nation. His statue dominates Prague's Old Town Square; the inscription reads: "Love the truth. Let others have their truth and truth will prevail."[11]

Havel's debt to Hus and other religious leaders is obvious. It is a deeply spiritual debt. As he looked at Czechoslovakia's recent past and what had gone wrong in their society Havel said, in his New Year's address:

We have become morally ill because we have become accustomed to saying one thing and doing another. We have learned not to believe in anything, not to care about one another and only to look after ourselves. Notions such as love, friendship, compassion, humility and forgiveness have lost their depth dimension.[12]

"Lost their depth dimension...." Havel might have said: "Lost their transcendence." For Havel does not call his people, or us, to a mere set of standards or values. Each individual, he says, is responsible to the "absolute horizon of Being." He speaks of a moment in the prison work camp when he was so totally filled with a sense of joy and well-being that he was "suddenly given a glimpse into the abyss of the infinite, of uncertainty, of mystery."

Havel would be the first to admit that this kind of vision is only given to us in glimpses and that it needs constantly to be translated into specific reforms. But the vision sustains us when we don't see the way, and his glimpse of it inspires all of us not to give up. Havel's eyes are on heaven, but his feet are placed firmly on the ground. "The only place to begin is with myself," he says. "It is I who must begin." And his time in prison made him realize the cost involved:

---

[11]See Richard Stranger, "Vaclav Havel: Heir to a Spiritual Legacy," *Christian Century*, April 11, 1990.
[12]Ibid.

Yes: [we are] in fact nailed down — like Christ on the Cross — to a grid of paradoxes.... [We] balance between the torment of not knowing [our] mission and the joy of carrying it out, between nothingness and meaningfulness. And like Christ, [we are] in fact victorious by virtue of [our] defeats.

Havel has known the power of evil against which we strive. He saw that power succeed for many years. In fact, both he and the Czech people — and all the world — were astonished at how quickly, all of a sudden, that evil power seemed to collapse. It was as if Havel was reading, as Jesus did, from one of the great prophecies with which he had grown up, and then said, as Jesus did to his people: "Today these sayings have come true in your very hearing."

Havel, like Jesus, does not speak of spiritual things in abstract terms. To be transcendent is not to be otherworldly. On the contrary, to be transcendent is to give ultimacy to truth, to base it on the eternal, not the temporal. Our society tends to think of values as "subjective," as personal preferences with no universal foundation. But the Czech reformers remember the famous statement of Tomáš Masaryk, the first president of Czechoslovakia: "Values, too, are facts." Why, they ask themselves in the face of the strong temptations to consumerism, should they hope to succeed in their vision? "I know of only one answer," says Kohak. "That the good is worth striving for simply because it is good." What a healthy antidote to our scientific approach to life! What a refreshing contrast to the concept that values are tested by their "benefits."

## Violence and the Reign of God

People like Havel, while visionaries, are not naive. They know that while the day of God's Reign may have dawned, the powers of darkness can well strike again. Peace is always challenged by war or violence of some sort. A strange saying of Jesus recognizes this human reality:

"From the days of John the Baptist until now the Kingdom of heaven has suffered violence, and the violent take it by force" (Matthew 11:12).

Luke's version is slightly different:

> "The law and the prophets were in effect until John came;
> since then the good news of the kingdom of God is pro-
> claimed, and everyone tries to enter it by force" (Luke
> 16:16).

Jesus remembered all too keenly that John the Baptist, his close
friend and fellow-prophet, was imprisoned and then beheaded for
his bold stand against the behavior of the king and queen. Jesus
realized that God enters human history in a time of conflict and
that defeat is as possible as victory. Paradoxically, violence and
peacemaking seem to exist together. "The outcome of the battle
may be sure, but the casualties are going to be real, not sham."[13]
We need to remember this warning, that violence "comes with
the territory" of God's Reign, so that, as we envision the future
and work out that vision, we are not surprised by the opposition. Bishop Tutu and Nelson Mandela need no such warning.
They know the violence of apartheid, and they know how those
who work for equality are violently suppressed, while the leaders
of apartheid have continued to call on the victims to "renounce
violence."

In North America, for example, we might think that, once dangers to the environment are made perfectly clear, everyone would
cooperate in trying to save it. With our pride in our technological
know-how, we might think that the proposed legislation to produce, by 1997, 750,000 vehicles fueled by something cleaner than
gasoline, for sale in badly polluted Southern California, would be
a stimulating challenge. Alas. Not so. The auto and oil industries
call this goal unattainable and lobby strongly against the proposal.
Similarly, a bill to cut back on coke production plants by the year
2020 is met by stiff opposition from the steel industry.

When smoking was proved to contribute to lung cancer, the tobacco lobbies spent millions trying to discredit the studies. They
vigorously opposed bills that required warnings on cigarette pack-
ages. And when smoking was prohibited in more and more places
and public opinion was swinging against the smoking habit, the
tobacco industries switched their promotion to countries where

---

[13]Norman Perrin, *Rediscovering the Teachings of Jesus* (New York: Harper &
Row, 1976), p. 77.

anti-smoking movements had not yet arisen. Violence and the Kingdom.

In Northern Quebec a huge hydro-electric development is under way. If it proceeds, a territory the size of France will be totally reshaped and the economic base of the ten thousand Crees who live there will be destroyed. The Crees insist that they retain their aboriginal rights with respect to the natural resources in this area; they demand that, at the very least, Hydro-Quebec needs federal and provincial authorization based on full environmental studies by both governments before the project proceeds. The whole area teems with wildlife and it is impossible, even with the best of studies, say many environmentalists, to predict what effect the massive flooding of hundreds of acres of land would ultimately have. Some studies have indeed been made but the government seems all too anxious to proceed. The project can bring billions of dollars to Quebec through export of electricity to neighboring New York and Vermont. Small wonder that many in Quebec might be willing to risk violence to the environment. But the Native peoples have been through such campaigns before. They are not as surprised as they used to be that their rights, and the rights of the environment, may well be violated.

## Expensive Wineskins

Jesus knows not only about the violence that the Reign of God encounters. He knows also about the cost it involves for those who choose to participate in it. Again and again he warns would-be followers:

> "No one who puts a hand to the plow and looks back is fit for the kingdom of God" (Luke 9:62).

> Enter through the narrow gate; for the gate is wide and the road is easy that leads to destruction, and there are many who take it. For the gate is narrow and the road is hard that leads to life, and there are few who find it" (Matthew 7:13–14; see also Matthew 16:24–26).

People like Vaclav Havel know what such sayings mean, for they have proven them in their own experience. The challenges facing many of us may be less dramatic but, in their own way, nonetheless real. If we are committed, for example, to cleaning up the environment — if we see that project as a new "wineskin" into which we pour the new "wine" of our vision of nature and humanity as parts of one community — it will cost each of us a considerable amount. It will cost money. Carl Sonnen, vice-president of Informetrica, says that on the basis of a study he made in 1989 it will cost Canadians at least $70.2 billion in new investment by the turn of the century just to implement environmental standards that already exist. "We should be asking," he says, "whether families are prepared to pay an average of $1,500 more a year, each year, for cleaner air and cleaner water."[14] (A recent poll showed that a majority would be willing to pay $100.)

But costs will be measured in more than money. Right now many projects, like the proposed Quebec hydro plan, are on hold, awaiting environmental studies. On the outcome hangs not only income for Quebec and a supply of electricity for New York and Vermont, but the potential for many jobs. Will people forego jobs for the sake of the environment? The same question applies to any commitment to peace and disarmament. What about the people whose livelihood depends on working in armament factories? Jobs often mean not only livelihood but people's very identity. A person without a job in our society is often a person without an identity. We have seen, in the case of Robert (above, p. 1), what a price is demanded of a person whose commitment to peace could mean loss of employment.

Similarly difficult questions are posed to farmers. Should they use chemical fertilizers and insecticides that pollute the environment? If not, crop yields will decrease and how then will they make a living? And what about our forest industry and the people who work in it? What do we ask of them in order to preserve the heritage of hundreds of years for the future of our planet?

And what do we do about our garbage? About the conservation of energy? On a per capita basis, Canadians are the world's most profligate users of energy, the largest producers of garbage, and the fourth-largest emitters of carbon dioxide. With similar consumption patterns, Americans are not far behind. Obviously, if we love this planet, we are going to have to make some

---

[14]Quoted in "The Cost of Going Green," *Maclean's*, April 30, 1990.

hard decisions not only in this decade but in the generations to come.[15]

But participating in the Reign of God and working toward it involves such difficult decisions, such high costs and such constant frustrations, as Jesus himself experienced. It is one thing to rejoice in the new appreciation of the environment, to celebrate a new relationship of humanity to nature. It is another thing to pay the cost of the celebration. As Jesus said:

> Which of you, intending to build a tower, does not first sit down and estimate the cost, to see whether you have enough to complete it? Otherwise, when you have laid a foundation and are not able to finish, all who see it will begin to ridicule you, saying, 'This person began to build and was not able to finish'" (Luke 14:28–30*).

Obviously, if we take seriously our conversion to the kind of relationship to nature we believe God originally intended, we will have to make some radical changes in the way we live. We will have to reorder our priorities according to that changed relationship. (We might add, of course, that the alternative course — to continue as we are — would, in the end, be even more costly.)

## Beyond Survival

Organizations and institutions must also struggle with this reordering. Let us think about the Christian church. We have rejoiced as we saw the way in which churches have often been leaders in the radical changes that have taken place in Europe. In Poland, the Roman Catholic church was for many years the official opposition to the communist government. In East Germany, churches (mainly Protestant) were often the places where people gathered to express their anger against the oppressive regime and their hopes for the future. In Romania, it was a pastor's insistence on conducting Christian education classes, daring to challenge the laws of the land, that sparked the people's uprising. And in Czechoslovakia, as we have seen, it was descendants of Jan Hus who provided the vision the people yearned for.[16]

---

[15]Ibid.

[16]See J. Martin Bailey, *The Spring of Nations: Churches in the Rebirth of Eastern Europe* (New York: Friendship Press, 1991).

But what of churches in the West? Do we use changes in Eastern Europe to gloat over "our victory" over "atheistic communism?" Or can we see that this is a time for serious re-examination of the church as it exists in democratic regimes? Do we attribute declining membership in the mainline churches merely to the growing secularism in society, or do we see a loss of transcendence in what is supposed to be the very place of transcendence? We may rejoice that the so-called Constantinian era of the church, the era in which the church became "the official religion of society," is over. But what are we putting in its place? Do we care more about techniques for institutional survival than the discovery of new wines to put in new wineskins? Do we merely wait for people to come back to church, or do we look for ways in which the church may "come back to the people?"

It is good for us in the church to be aware of how much the church has adapted to our culture and accepted its values. We have worshipped bigness, accepted a secular concept of progress, condoned the violation of nature, baptized discrimination against women and accepted with alacrity hierarchical systems of ministry that leave lay people passive. For all this we need to repent, not only to God but to one another and the world. For the task given to us is to be the leaven in the lump, not just a part of the lump. The vocation to which we are called is to be part of the creative tension between culture as it is and society as it could be. Our community is to be unique in cutting across all divisions of class and race, but we have reflected all too accurately the divisions of society.

## The Reign Among Us

Christianity in North America has become essentially a middle-class religion. Some churches, notably black, Hispanic, Roman Catholic and Pentecostal, include different classes and races. But many church services are perceived as irrelevant, elitist, incomprehensible or just plain boring.

People are by nature religious. Many people today deeply long for spiritual food to nourish them in their day-to-day lives. They wonder why, if they do go to church, they find little recognition of their weariness, their inner doubt and confusion, their profound thirst and hunger.

Is it time for the churches to repent for having failed their

God and their people? To be willing to sacrifice their pride, their institutions, their traditional place of privilege in the community, and to pray to God for a new vision of the gospel? To listen once more to the call of Christ to take up their cross, not for the sake of saving the life of the churches, but for the sake of saving the life of the world? Such listening might be very costly indeed. But it might mean rediscovering the meaning of the Reign of God.

Churches who discover the meaning of the Reign of God usually pay a price, but they also discover a new kind of joy. A church in an upper-middle-class neighborhood was shocked to discover that its beloved pastor had AIDS. A meeting of the congregation was called to decide how to respond. The facts of the situation were described openly. The pastor was too ill to return to work. He had possibly six months to a year to live. He had a wife and two children. What should the congregation do?

They decided, first of all, to assure the pastor and his family of their support and their prayers. His salary would be continued and the manse provided as long as it was needed. Provision would be made for Sunday preaching, but the members of the congregation would undertake the remainder of the pastor's duties. Finally, they decided that they would not hide their situation from anyone but that they would regard it as an opportunity to show that AIDS was an illness that could be faced openly. That would be part of the mission of their church.

Some months later, the pastor died and a new one arrived. In the meantime, the congregation had discovered that if they were to be pastors to each other and witnesses in the community they needed much more study, study of the Bible and of their faith. They prepared a mission statement to clarify their own goals and to help the new pastor understand the kind of leadership they were looking for. In the statement they said they were looking for a pastor who would challenge the congregation to risk taking the gospel seriously. Virtually all members testified that they had experienced a new vision of what it meant to be a Christian and what it meant to be a church. It had been a costly, and joyful, experience. They had participated, in their own way, in the Reign of God.

They were also excited to discover the truth of Jesus' statement that "the Reign of God is among you." It is possible to be looking so hard for the Reign of God or to be so frustrated in trying to define it that we miss examples of it near at hand.

## A Passionate People

C. S. Song, an Asian theologian, talks about a Zen monk in ancient China who painted ten cow-herding pictures to illustrate stages of spiritual progress. The first picture is called: "Looking for the Cow." The inscription says: "The cow has never been lost. It is the cowherd that is lost."

Song urges us to open our eyes and see the faith that has never been lost, present in the life and death struggles of people all around us. When people tell their own life stories we hear tales of passion, a passion expressed in a love that compels them, a love that leads to suffering. This suffering, says Song, creates communion. It is the cow that has never been lost. "But it takes a theological mind compelled by suffering love to know it."[17]

Few people within or without the church have connected their inner stories with the story of the faith. They do not see the Bible as part of their story; they do not see their struggle as part of the biblical struggle. They do not see their suffering as part of God's suffering. If the church could help them make that connection it would already have preached a great gospel.

If the church could hallow people's deepest questions, echo their heartfelt cries, that would be good news. To do so does not make the church a mere reflection of humanity. Instead, it means the church hallows the lives of God's people by lifting up their experience in the worship of God. It affirms their holy origins and draws their best hopes into the vision of God's Reign.

Just as we spoke of a new internationalism superseding outmoded nationalisms, we can begin to talk about a new kind of community open to all who wish to join. If the Reign of God is a foretaste of heaven, then, like heaven, it is all-inclusive. That is what Jesus envisioned and practiced. In the way he so easily ate with scribes and pharisees one day and with publicans and sinners the next, he infuriated those who wished to be exclusive. He disregarded the divisions that had kept people comfortable "with their own kind" — a spiritual and moral apartheid. Jesus

---

[17]C. S. Song, "Theology That Tells People's Passion Stories," *HES Theological Education*, 1984, p. 33.

celebrated the Kingdom by transcending such divisions. He spoke with enthusiasm of that great day in the Kingdom when people from all corners of the earth would gather together. In a parable he described a wedding feast where those invited made excuses not to come, so the host went out into the city streets and country lanes and invited as many as he could find, both bad and good. "So the wedding hall was filled with guests" (see Matthew 22:1–10).

Christians do not need to look far for a vocation in this confused and rapidly changing world. Their calling, their vision is already pictured in the great banquet that includes all who will come. It remains for the church to become the new wineskin into which this wine, so new to most people, can be poured. In transcending the divisions that society still clings to, and in humbly listening to the life stories of the humblest, hearing in them echoes of "the word of God," the church becomes an outpost of God's Reign. Then the church shows itself a living symbol of what "is to be" instead of a reflection of what "is." To believe that and to act accordingly creates tensions that at times are deeply painful, but at other times highly exhilarating.

Best of all, we discover the joy of participating in God's Reign and in the self-fulfillment that comes with such participation. Instead of fearing our deaths because they mark the end of our lives, we become part of a community that began long before us and will live long after us. We embrace that "abundant life," that "eternal life," that Jesus spoke of.

## Glimpses of God's Reign

Many of us have had inklings of that kind of fulfillment. I recall traveling to New York City, some years ago, to participate in a great peace rally. By some estimates, a million people were there. I will never forget emerging from the subway and seeing that great phalanx of people coming up the street. It was not just the sheer numbers that inspired me. It was the wide variety. People of all colors and races were moving together. There were Buddhist monks from Japan and Christian ministers from North America. There were labor unions and associations of every kind. Best of all, there seemed to be no specialists or experts in the crowd or, if there were, they could not be singled out. Elderly men and women with canes held signs like "Grandparents for Peace." Young mothers pushed baby carriages holding signs: "Don't let our children die." But all were marching against one thing: war. All were marching for one thing: peace. That made us all one. That made us all feel we were part of a community greater than any one person or class or race. All of us knew that we might be naive to believe that lasting peace would come in our lifetimes. But we felt we were participating in a cause based in eternity, a cause that transcended any merely human life or organization. I felt a great surge of fulfillment in life. I felt part of the Kingdom.

In the spring of 1990 I happened to be in New York again and had a similar experience, although in quite different circumstances. A play of Vaclav Havel's was being presented. *Audience* depicted a dissident author in conversation with a brewmaster, his boss. In the play, neither the writer nor the brewmaster could speak openly to each other, a typical situation in Czechoslovakia before its liberation.

Following Havel's play was a brief one-act work by Samuel Beckett. *Catastrophe* was written as a tribute to Havel in 1981 when Havel was serving a four-and-a-half-year prison term for being a founding signatory of "Charter 77," which asserted that the "fundamental rights of man existed only on paper in Czechoslovakia."

In Beckett's play, a director and his assistant arrange the posture of a young man standing on a plinth, like a statue. The director dictates how he should be left shivering in his pajamas with his head bowed and his hair hiding his face.

Originally, the play had ended with that humiliation. Beckett had depicted the plight of freedom-loving people in the Czechoslovakia of the early 1980s. But Beckett had died four days before Havel's dramatic inauguration as president of Czechoslovakia. The New York director felt he could not let the play end as Beckett had written it. He added a short piece: the young man, shivering on the plinth, slowly raises his head, throws back his hair and stands upright. Meantime, the Czech anthem surges to a crescendo.

The audience rose and clapped. We were not just watching a play. We had participated in the death and resurrection of a great man of our day. We had seen defeat become victory. We had seen faith become reality. We had had a glimpse of God's Reign.

## The Great Banquet

Not all deaths and resurrections are that dramatic, of course. But they can be just as real. A church in a West Coast North American city had served a typical middle-class congregation. But in time that area of the city changed drastically. The middle-class people moved out. The poor and the homeless moved in. The church could have died and, in one form, it did. But it rose in another form. It opened its doors to everyone, especially the handicapped, the hungry, the transient, the prostitutes.

And they all came. Why? Because, as one of them put it, "I feel comfortable in this church. There's no stigma here, or if there is, people just keep it to themselves. So I just go about and be with everybody else and, you know, it feels good."[18] He was perennially on welfare, could not keep a job or maintain a relationship. But he was made welcome, asked to play his guitar and sing his songs in church, even asked to preach the sermon one evening. He was asked for his ideas. He said that on Sunday mornings when all the soup kitchens were closed, a lot of the men on the street had no place to go for something hot to eat. He suggested a porridge line. They put him in charge of it.

He understands the feelings of street people and the spiritual resources they need: "I think people need subconsciously to know there's a God, or need to know they're a part of the world and they have every bloody right to be here. You feel you have no place to be in God's world, and this is God's world."[19] He believes he has found such a place in this church. He is a testimony to, and a part of, a church that has caught a glimpse of the Reign of God and come alive.

We need not be unfeeling frogs sitting passively in a pot of water while we are boiled to death for our insensitivity. Nor need we be unwitting celebrants of a passing moment of victory, like the jubilant but condemned tail gunner in that ill-fated plane in the Second World War. Rather, we are like those people in Jesus' parable, ordinary and unknown people who live in the unnamed streets and lanes of life, who have been invited, to our eternal surprise, to the great banquet of the Reign of God. There we feast

---

[18]*Speaking for Themselves: Hearing the Gospel from the Dispossessed, the Undervalued and the Marginalized* (Toronto: United Church Publishing House, and Nashville: Abingdon Press, 1990), p. 20.

[19]Ibid, p. 21.

at the table that includes people of all sorts and conditions, as surprised as we are at being there, and we converse with the great Proclaimer of the Kingdom, Jesus Christ. And drink with him the new wine poured from new wineskins.

# *Where do our values lead us?*

L ATE ONE SATURDAY EVENING in April 1990, an Anglican priest, Michael Lapsley, returned to his home in Harare, Zimbabwe. He had attended a farewell party in his honor, hosted by friends who wished him well as he prepared to move to another assignment in Bulawayo, the second city of Zimbabwe.

He had been away on a speaking tour and quite a bit of mail had accumulated. As Lapsley started to sort through it, suddenly there was a loud explosion. A parcel bomb left Lapsley bleeding helplessly on the floor. Friends rushed him to the hospital in time to save his life but he lost both hands and one eye. He was badly deafened and had wounds all over his body. A close friend, who hosted the farewell party, wrote to tell of the tragic incident. He said: "He's recovering very well — in part a tribute to the care he's getting and even more to his indomitable spirit and faith in the God of justice."

"God of justice?" What kind of justice is it when a person dedicated to the struggle of South African blacks for freedom is left maimed for life by people who work for white supremacy and power? But Lapsley was not merely a victim of their hatred. He had made a choice and had counted the cost.

It was not an easy choice. Lapsley was born and brought up in New Zealand. As a child he read books like Trevor Huddleston's *Naught for your Comfort* and was deeply moved by the accounts of brutality against the blacks in South Africa.

In 1973, the religious order to which Lapsley belonged, the Society of Sacred Mission, sent him to South Africa to serve as a university chaplain to three campuses, two black and one white. At this time Lapsley was a strong pacifist. He used to argue with black students to persuade them that it was better for them to use nonviolent tactics to end apartheid. Then they would ask him where he was going to sleep. He had to answer: in his white suburb.

In 1976 came the Soweto uprising. More than a thousand students died in the streets before the end of the year. By this time Lapsley had become an outspoken critic of apartheid and, refused South African citizenship, was expelled from the country. He went to live in Lesotho, but even before leaving he had decided to join the African National Congress. He joined because he believed in the ANC goal of establishing a nonracial, democratic, unitary state. He joined also, as he said, "because I had concluded that the work of individuals would not end, nor was it an ultimate threat to, the apartheid state. Apartheid would end, and liberation would come, through people acting in concert in a disciplined and principled way as part of a vast movement."

In December 1982, while Lapsley was away from Lesotho for a short time, the South African army came and killed forty-two refugees and Lesotho citizens, including some secondary school children and babies. They were part of the community where Lapsley had lived. "Together we had shared hopes for a new life where children would sleep peacefully and grow up with pride and dignity without fear," said Lapsley. That incident was a turning point in his life.

"I made a vow that day," said Lapsley later, "that my life would be dedicated to ending apartheid and building a new society. What else could I offer my friends who had made the ultimate sacrifice and given me a taste of a new society where it is possible to be human and not black or white?"[1]

That vow has now been put to the test. Michael Lapsley had chosen his values and given his heart to them. He illustrates clearly for us that values do come from our faith, and that to believe in something is not merely to have an opinion about it. It is to commit one's whole self to it.

---

[1] From an article written for Canadian Universities Overseas Services' annual publication, *The Journal*, reprinted in *Toronto Globe and Mail*, May 1, 1990.

## Necessary Transcendence

Lapsley knew that to commit oneself to a cause one believes to be part of the Realm of God is no guarantee of success. Our values, based on our love of a God of justice, will not necessarily become the values of our society. Many times we will wonder if we have made a mistake. Often we will be lonely, feeling we are the "odd person out." But that puts us in the company of the prophets down through the centuries.

Lapsley's decision to worship a God who was the God of blacks and whites made him strive to treat all people as persons. He saw how a lesser god, a god for one race or class only, was an idol. Only the God above gods gave him the transcendent perspective to see the idolatry of apartheid. Worship of this God also gave him a higher view of himself. He could not be defined as white, nor could others be defined as black. Both were made in the image of God. Both were human beings. Nobody, then, could treat blacks as mere servants or laborers. Both oppressors and oppressed had to be liberated: the oppressed from bondage to their oppressors, and the oppressors from bondage to a god that favored one race over another.

Because we are not directly involved in the struggle against apartheid, it is easier to see the idolatry of that system. It is not so easy to see the idolatries in societies that seem to be more open and free. Yet we are in bondage to a form of materialism that treats people as "markets" and shapes our wants to serve its profits. Both businesses and buyers need to see themselves as children of God first, lest they become mere "profit makers" and "consumers."

We keep being driven back to the importance of our belief in a transcendent God. Only a God who transcends the labeling of people as worthless or as things, whether that labeling be done by us or others, can give us a vision of ourselves and others as children of God. Only a God who transcends the sinfulness of each of us and of our society can inspire us with a vision of a world where the bondage to possessions is broken. Only a God who gives us a picture of what things should be can allow us to face squarely how things are. Only such a God can point us in the direction we should go.

Only a transcendent God can lift us from despair about ourselves and our world. The Bible continually returns to this theme. We saw it in God's covenant with Noah after God regretted destroying the earth in his despair. It is such a covenant with imperfect people that allows us to hope that our world can yet be redeemed, to believe that in fact we are constantly being redeemed.

### Bearers of Hope

I saw this kind of faith when I visited Nicaragua in 1985. Along the Coco River, which borders Honduras, had lived settlements of Miskito Indians. The Nicaraguan "contras," many of them Miskitos as well, had encampments just across this border and used to attack frequently. The Nicaraguan government, to protect the Miskitos on "their" side, moved them back from the border. But in so doing, they also moved them away from their beloved Coco River, their traditional home. The Miskitos were desperately unhappy and the government realized they had no option but to move them back.

This task was costly and very dangerous because bands of armed guerillas still moved freely in the area. The return could not take place with any safety unless some movement to make peace with the rebels also took place. Who could undertake the challenge?

The government asked Myrna Cunningham, a Miskito Indian. It was not easy for her to respond. She is a medical doctor, a very good one. Should she leave the work that was so needed and which she so enjoyed? More than that, why should she make peace with the rebels? She herself had once been captured by them, tortured and raped. Should she now negotiate with them?

But Myrna Cunningham is a committed Christian and she loves her people. She said yes. She undertook the complex task of moving the Miskitos back to their river, and she talked with any of the enemy who would talk to her. In the few days we were in the area, the rebels blew up two trucks on their way to transport people back to their homes. We could see that Myrna Cunningham was upset, but there was no thought of giving up. In fact, she offered her job as mediator to one of the rebel leaders if he would commit himself to the task of peacemaking.

She was under no illusions about the obstacles between her goal and the facts of the situation, but her commitment was unshakeable. I will never forget Myrna Cunningham's round smiling face, a face filled with love, forgiveness, faith and courage, a symbol of the Reign of God already present.

Cynicism is common in our world and believers in God, as well as others, can often succumb to it. But believers in the God of hope cannot remain cynical. That is a contradiction in faith. Our nature and our vocation is to hope and to be bearers of hope to a despairing world.

## Bones That Rise

The prophet Ezekiel can inspire us here. In fact, his situation bears certain similarities to Myrna Cunningham's. Because of a war, his people were exiles in a strange land, Babylon. Though their lot was not hard, they longed to return to their beloved homeland, to Jerusalem and to its beautiful temple. But there seemed no hope of that happening; the powers against them were invincible. They gave way to despair.

But then Ezekiel had a vision (Ezekiel 37:1–14). He saw a broad plain strewn with human bones, white and dry in the sun. God asked him: "Mortal, can these bones live again?"[2] Ezekiel would not presume to answer such a question. "O Lord God, you know," he replied. But God had asked the crucial question, the one in the hearts of all the people. Is there any hope? Or is this the end?

"Can these bones live again?" That is the question of our day, too. In such rapidly changing times, when the foundations of faith and our world are shaken, is there any hope? As we look out over the plain littered with dry bones of slaughtered values, it is tempting to avoid that question.

We could analyze the situation and tell why the tragic massacre occurred. We could count the bones and estimate the number of victims. We could study the scene of battle and suggest what strategies were used, who won and who lost. We could suggest what use could be made of the bones. We could study the value of the property, obviously so inefficiently used, and what could profitably be erected on it.

But God does not ask for analyses or studies or proposals. God asks: "Can these bones live again?" "Is there any hope?" When

---

[2]Some translations say "Man" or "Mortal Man" or "Son of Man."

Ezekiel declines to answer, God commands him to speak to the bones and tell them that God will breathe new life in them. God then tells Ezekiel to command the wind, the spirit, to breathe into the slain and revive them. Trembling, Ezekiel obeys, and the dead rise, a mighty army.

The vision speaks directly to the dispirited people. They say: "Our bones are dried up, and our hope is lost; we are cut off completely" ("our thread of life is snapped, our web is severed from the loom," NEB). But God says to them: "I will put my spirit into you and you shall live."

## Enabled Communities

It takes courage to preach God's message of renewed life to a world that accepted the Cold War as a permanent institution, the death of millions of children a year as "normal," the division of the world into rich and poor as "inevitable" and the preaching of hope as "naiveté." But those are the attitudes and conditions we are called to challenge. The hope we preach cannot be based on scientific or historical evidence. It can be based only on a faith in a God who loves this world and who never stops loving it. A God who continues to make covenants with people who break them. A God who continually brings order out of chaos, light out of darkness, justice out of injustice and love out of hate. This is the God who never stops valuing this world and who constantly calls us to value it with God. Only in our belief in such a God do we find value in ourselves and in our society.

But to hold this faith as individuals is not enough. While God made each of us as unique persons, God also set us in communities. The story of our creation in Genesis 1 says: "God said, 'Let us make humankind in our image' ...male and female God created them" (vv. 26, 27*). Genesis seems to be speaking of the creation of a species, not a collection of independent individuals. Genesis 2:7 says: "the Lord God formed man from the dust of the ground." The word translated "humankind" in Genesis 1:26 and "man" in Genesis 2:7 is the same in Hebrew: *adam*. *Adam* is a play on the Hebrew word *adamah*, which means "earth." In English we might say, as Phyllis Trible suggests, that God made "humans," a play on the word *humus*, which in Latin means "earth" or "ground."

We are called, then, not only to accept ourselves as individually made in the image of God but as a community made to commune with each other and with God. Never is this more important than when we contemplate the difficulty of making those lonely choices that go against the majority and leave us feeling ridiculed and discredited. When he answered God's call, the prophet Isaiah was told that he would be left like a mere stump of a tree. But that stump would be "the holy seed" that held the hope of the future.

It takes courage and faith to believe this promise, but such faith forms real community. My friend, writing to tell me about the tragic maiming of Michael Lapsley, speaks about the "base community" that used to meet at Lapsley's house. There this small group shared their faith and their ideas and plans. They celebrated the Eucharist together. When they heard what had happened, many were angry and afraid. When will it end? they asked. Who will be next?

"And yet," wrote my friend, "out of this [incident] formed a community of people, very disparate and diverse: ANC exiles from South Africa, young disaffected blacks from the Harare townships, expatriates like me and others, whites, blacks, Christians, atheists, nonbelievers, affluent and poor. We are united by Michael's courage and faith, his unwavering commitment to bring an end to apartheid, his solid faith, his humor and also his outbursts of anger against the Boers, his challenging of himself and wondering about a God who says we must suffer all the time for what that God has told us is right — peace and justice."

Not many of us face the critical situation of Michael Lapsley and his friends or of Myrna Cunningham and the Miskito community. But the principle is the same. Like Sandra who came to that discussion/study group, we need places for people to share their doubts and their tentative beliefs. We need core groups within congregations who will covenant with one another to wrestle over their difficult choices together and support one another in those choices. We need groups who will ask: "What can we do together that we cannot do as individuals?" We need groups who will share a common foundation for their faith but understand that individuals may come to different decisions as to how to build on that foundation. Michael Lapsley, for example, felt that in his situation he had to give up his pacifist stance. Mahatma Gandhi and Martin Luther King, on the other hand, while believing in the same God of love, chose nonviolent ways.

People who are harassed with unavoidable responsibilities need ways to do what they can. Many congregations provide tables in their after-service coffee hours where special causes are promoted. At such tables people can get literature to inform them, offer what time they can afford, sign a petition or give money. Some may be able to write letters on behalf of prisoners of conscience for Amnesty International. Some may undertake to write or telephone shut-ins or people going through difficult times of bereavement or divorce. Others may find time to care for a mentally handicapped person, even for a few hours, to give the person's family some respite.

Such things, by themselves, seem small. But all are ways of contributing to the community of faith, the community that is concerned for the work of God's Reign. We are reminded by Jesus himself that whoever gives even a cup of cold water to the needy in his name is important.

## God of the Mountains

Nor should we forget that participation in God's work is not confined to "action." I recall being in Berlin in 1960 just before the Berlin wall was erected. A trickle of people were fleeing East Germany and arriving in Berlin. I asked the director of a center sponsored by the churches for such refugees: "What can we do to help?" I expected her to speak about political action or about sending material aid such as money, blankets or clothing. But she replied without hesitation: "What we need most is informed prayer." The church can be a source of information and inspire us to pray accordingly.

As we pray, we become aware that we are a part of a worldwide praying community. This helps us feel we are not alone in our concern for global issues like the care of the environment. It helps us, when we lose battles in our own region or nation, to know that those losses are not the whole picture nor the final verdict.

In our prayers God can help us as we try to choose among values that arouse conflict within ourselves as well as within our communities. Again and again we will be required to choose between the gods who represent particular interests or limited goals and the God who transcends those interests and goals.

Pablo Richard, a biblical scholar from Chile, discusses the Hebrews' decision to make a golden calf to worship while Moses was on the mountain talking with God. He says they chose the god of the plains instead of the God of the mountains. That temptation faces us constantly. As the Hebrews were tempted to choose a visible god that they could see and touch and even shape to their own liking, so it will be tempting for us to choose values that are tangible and achievable and adapted to our situation and our interests.

Such gods may not be evil; they merely may not be lofty enough. They may suit our immediate needs but they may not lead us to something, someone greater. We need the God of the mountaintop, a God who is invisible but who calls us beyond ourselves. It takes great faith and courage to follow a God who cannot be seen and who leads us to a "Promised Land" that we can barely imagine. But any God who is less than that is not a God we could ultimately worship or follow for long. It is not the God who called Moses and Isaiah, Ruth and Mary Magdalene, Young Kim and Vaclav Havel, Michael Lapsley and Myrna Cunningham.

### Twisted Bikes

We worship the God who calls us to share the vision of God's own Reign. Such a vision, Jesus assures us, does not reside in some unimaginable future. The Reign of God, while always in the future, is also always present, always "in the midst" of us. Jesus calls us to look for evidence of God's Reign among us. Such evidence is not only cause for "optimism"; it is proof of God's activity in God's world and in God's people.

When we think of the environment, for example, we see not only the violence that continues to be done to it. We see change. We see signs of repentance. In Brazil, where the destruction of the Amazon forests affects the whole planet, the government showed little concern or responsibility for what was happening. But then a new government appointed an environmentalist to implement a forest conservation program. Even before that government appointment, Brazilian television took a hand. An imaginative and concerned TV writer visited the Pantanal, the world's largest wetland. The writer decided to create a "soap opera" in which, he said, "the Pantanal itself would be a character, because it changes people so much." The program reaches an estimated forty million viewers, not least of whom is the president himself. While we rail against the blindness of governments and the superficiality of television, we need to note that the Reign of God can be among them too, and rejoice.

We can rejoice, too, in visions like that of the Dalai Lama of Tibet. The day after he received the Nobel Prize he gave a little-noticed speech in Stockholm. He described himself as a "simple monk" and suggested that for the good of the people of Tibet and of the world in general Tibet might be transformed into what he called a Zone of Ahisma. *Ahisma,* a word from the nonviolent Jain religion, means "non-harm." The Dalai Lama conceives of a Zone of non-harming, or of peace, with three levels: "peace among human beings by the transformation of the Tibetan plateau into a militarily neutral zone; peace between humanity and other species by turning Tibet into 'the world's largest natural park' . . .; peace between humanity and the earth by forbidding technologies that produce hazardous wastes."[3]

When we realize that Tibet is now one of the most militarized countries in the world, occupied by at least 250,000 Chinese troops; when we note that it is the site of atomic testing, that its people are under the heel of Beijing's ruthless regime; when we see how the Chinese are ravaging the forests and mining the sacred mountains, we wonder how anyone could even fantasize about creating an Ahisma, a peaceful, nonviolent zone, there.

But Tibet used to be that kind of country, based on the Buddhist compassion for all living beings. And when we think of the astounding and unpredicted events in Eastern Europe we may be more open to the possibility of "the impossible" coming to pass.

Even when we consider the violent crushing of the spirited democratic uprising in China, we feel that we have seen a glimpse of the Reign of God among us. Will we ever forget that moment on television when we watched a single student stop a whole column of tanks in Tiananmen Square? As we look to the future, will we bet on the tanks that rolled over the students and crushed

[3]See the article by George Woodcock, a Vancouver author who has known the Dalai Lama for almost thirty years, in the *Toronto Globe and Mail,* April 11, 1990.

their bodies along with their bikes, or will we bet on the dream of the martyrs? If we were sculptors, would we choose as our model an unscathed tank or a twisted bike?

## Today's Martyrs

A temptation that too easily seduces us says: "Martyrs all lived in bygone ages. People today aren't sufficiently committed to die for their faith, even if the occasion presented itself." Yielding to such a temptation can be used as an excuse for half-hearted commitment to the Reign of God, or for ignoring the many examples of martyrdom in our time.

But consider, for example, four Roman Catholic women missionaries who went from the U.S. to El Salvador. Maura Clarke, Ita Ford, Jean Donovan and Dorothy Kazel had gone on a "mission of accompaniment." This is how they described it: "to search out the missing, pray with families of prisoners, bury the dead, and work with the people in their struggle to break out of the bonds of oppression, poverty and violence." On December 2, 1980, Dorothy Kazel and Jean Donovan drove to the San Salvador airport to meet Ita Ford and Maura Clarke, who had been at a conference in Nicaragua. When the four women left the airport, their van was stopped and a military guardsman took over the driver's seat. The van followed a National Guard jeep to an isolated spot about fifteen miles from the airport. There, all four women were raped and shot.

Was their work lost or in vain? Nine years later, six Jesuit priests, teachers at a San Salvador university, their housekeeper and her daughter were similarly gunned down. Has nothing changed? Is the work of such people futile?

Ten years after the murder of the missionary women, the Religious Task Force on Central America devoted an issue of its journal to a reflection on what these four women have left us. It spoke of

> a legacy of incarnated faith.... [They] showed us Christ immediately present in this world, in a concrete people, in the suffering and death, and in the profound hope, of the poor.... They put power back into the Gospel for many of us, a Gospel that had become disempowered by the same cultural values that affect the whole society.... [They inspired

people who] work for change, the slow, deliberate, often frustrating work of changing people in *this* country, challenging our values, witnessing our faith, and confronting the policies that reflect the spirit of death rather than of life....

They also helped us rediscover our ability to "vision" a future, not only to denounce, but to point to where we are going. This is essential if we are not to end in despair. The new creation of God has values and goals, and our faith language makes it possible for us to talk about it, point to it, empowering us with hope.[4]

The journal went on to say that these four women had demonstrated what happens when ordinary people are called on to do extraordinary things in faith. "Finally," it concludes, "they leave us a moving and powerful legacy about the dignity, giftedness, and the prophetic role of women in the church....[They] should resolve for all time any question about whether or not women can completely 'image' Christ in our world."

## Visions and Songs

C. S. Song tells how cicadas' eggs hatch in a tree and fall to the ground where they burrow in the soil.[5] It takes three to seventeen years for them to mature. Then they have only a few weeks of life — to mate and die. So they must sing! So we, in our brief span of life here on earth, must find a song to sing.

It cannot be merely a song of the times. We live in such changing times. We cannot be satisfied to sing the latest hit, to follow the latest fad. We need "a living song," a song that will outlive our times, though we sing it here and now. It must be a song of the ages, a song of the past, the present and the future. Otherwise we will feel that our lives, and the choices we made, are of little account. Where can we find such a song?

It may be found in the Revelation to John. The writer has been imprisoned for his faith, for his decision not to worship the ruler — the god — of the Roman empire. He had chosen, with other Christians, to worship the God of Jesus Christ, a radically different God. There is no indication that he will be released nor

[4]Margaret Swedish, "Harvesting the Legacy," *Central America Report*, 1990.
[5]C. S. Song, "Theology That Tells People's Passion Stories," *HES Theological Education*, 1984.

that the little band of Christians will survive the terrible persecution they were undergoing. They are under great pressure to worship the approved gods, to adopt the values of the majority. The writer knows their sufferings and hears their cry: How long, O Lord, how long? But he also hears shouts of victory and blasts of trumpets and songs of joy as he sees beyond their bleeding wounds. In one place he describes a vision he has of "those who had won the victory over the beast and its image," the false gods of the Roman empire. "They sing the song of Moses, the servant of God, and the song of the Lamb":

> Great and amazing are your deeds,
>     Lord God, the Almighty!
> Just and true are your ways,
>     King of the nations!
> Lord, who will not fear
>     and glorify your name?
> For you alone are holy.
>     All nations will come
>     and worship before you,
> for your judgments have been revealed.
>                 (Revelation 15:3–4)

While this song may sound rather "triumphalistic" in our day, we can imagine the hope it would give the tiny minority of persecuted Christians in that day. In this vision they could see that the Kingdom, in a mysterious way, was very real and very present.

Michael Lapsley's sister, speaking for her brother while he lay in his hospital bed, said: "Michael wants me to say today that through such acts against the poor and the defenseless, apartheid is unmasked. . . . My brother ends by saying that his own commitment as a priest [and] as a Christian . . . has only been strengthened and made more resolute by what has been done to him." It sounds like a song from the Revelation to John.

Jesus, as we have noted, made difficult choices. Right to the very end, the choices did not get any easier. Yet he chose to seek daily the presence and guidance of God, finding in that search more courage and faith than through any safe and sure way. To him, it was more important to be a part of the work of God's

Reign and to delight in the signs of its presence than to achieve any goals he might have conceived by himself.

In his spirit his followers wrote:

> Therefore, since we are surrounded by so great a cloud of witnesses, let us also lay aside every weight and the sin that clings so closely, and let us run with perseverance the race that is set before us, looking to Jesus, the pioneer and perfecter of our faith, who for the sake of the joy that was set before him, endured the cross, disregarding its shame (Hebrews 12:1–2).

I remember Robert, who stayed to talk with me after a meeting and who agonized over his decision to work on a project for Star Wars. When I saw his agony I apologized for having made life so hard for him by speaking so often about Star Wars in our worship services. Perhaps, I said, it was not fair to hold out such a difficult vision. Perhaps I should have been more realistic, appreciated more how things really are than talk about how they should be. But at that statement, Robert looked even more anguished. On the verge of tears he said: "But don't you see? That's why we come to church in the first place!"